The

WINNING IMAGE

James Gray, Jr.

amacom

P9-DGG-637

AMERICAN MANAGEMENT ASSOCIATION

#7947635

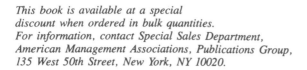

Library of Congress Cataloging in Publication Data

*Gray, James, 1945-
  The winning image.*

  *Includes index.
  1. Success.   I. Title   II. Title: Image.
  BF637.S8G69   650.1'.3   81-69372
  ISBN 0-8144-5667-7   AACR2
  ISBN 0-8144-7611-2 pbk*

Printing number

10 9 8 7 6 5 4 3 2

Preface

Young professionals on the rise and seasoned executives alike recognize the need to convey a professional image. Successful business executives and professionals know that how they look and act influences their personal success and the success of their corporation. As we go about our everyday business we rub elbows with many types of people in many types of situations, from a talk with the boss to a presentation before several thousand corporate shareholders. It's just natural to want to know how our overall appearance and style affect other people's perceptions of us.

That's why you will find this book of value. As an adjunct professor at The American University in Washington, D.C., I created a course in refining and enhancing personal image, a course that combines aspects of public relations, management, media relations, public speaking, body language, and the use of video. Directed mainly at executives, the seminar version of the course has met with great success among corporation executives, government professionals, attorneys, broadcasters, salesmen, and business entrepreneurs.

As an integral part of my public relations practice, I am a consultant on image. I've worked privately with men and women in Congress and with leaders in business and government. I have led seminars for corporations and government agencies.

I invite you to share my experience and to see how image can help you win your bid for greater success. Many of the problems—*and their solutions*—that grew out of my work with clients are shared here. This is the first reason you'll find this book unique: It combines practical business cases with proven principles of business communication. A second reason you'll find this book unique is the "what to do and how to do it" approach, the approach through situation, which allows you to apply on the job what you learn here. A third reason you'll find this book unique is the attention to detail: It shows how the small, subtle things that might ordinarily be overlooked are important. From experience we know that the subtleties of *how* we communicate are just as important as *what* we communicate.

I have applied a building block approach to this book. Each section builds on the previous and leads into the next. You may want to read one or another section first for immediate use. But to maximize the usefulness of the book, you should read all of it and get a grasp of the total picture of image.

Part I defines the concept of image and examines it as a growing trend in the world around us, among both men and women in politics and corporate life. This section stresses the importance of image for the professional on the move.

Part II treats enhancement of image, beginning with self-image, proceeding to use of dress and color to accommodate your particular physical make-up, and then to the importance of gestures, posture, and the vocal image. These are the primary ingredients of the total impression you project. Practical information is included so that you will know how to improve your image. A special note: these topics are treated individually by entire books, many of them psychological. What is presented here is focused specifically for professionals and executives and the problems they encounter, based on interviews with respected authorities, studies, research, and discussions with professionals themselves.

Part III focuses on image inside the corporation—how to use your image to get better results when handling everyday business. It ranges from leading meetings and working with peers and subordinates to appearing on video and meeting the press, and it concludes with the social image of the corporate executive.

Part IV takes a brief look at techniques of self-promotion—how to make business contacts and turn them into clients or job contacts, how to put together stationery, and how to design a business card. Finally, a summary of hints gathers information about proper image in a job interview.

An investment in self-improvement is an investment as important as any you may make in the market. What you put into it should give you a substantial return.

James Gray, Jr.

Contents

Part I

THE CONCEPT OF IMAGE

What Is Image and How Can It Help You Succeed?

Impression, style, charisma, personality, salesmanship, call it what you wish—image is the way others see you, and it often determines how they treat you.

Inside or outside the corporation, image is important. Each business day you are called upon to guide activities in which image can determine the outcome—reporting to your department, making a presentation to the board of directors, speaking about your company to clubs or civic groups, making the strongest impression in a job interview, giving a sales pitch. In the office, at home, in any business or social setting, you impart a mental picture that others recognize and remember. This picture determines their reactions to you. Whether you have lunch with a new client or an interview for a job, whether you deal with employee problems or play golf with your favorite partner, each person you deal with reacts to your image. They see you as persuasive or ineffectual, assertive or passive, domineering or dominated, powerful or powerless, ready to confront a task or eager to avoid it.

Your image includes some of your inherent qualities. Your job is to make sure that your image identifies you with your best and strongest attributes. "You can't judge a book by its cover" expresses a widely held feeling about image. Many people think that it's difficult to judge another person by outward appearance. Their argument is that anyone with enough money to buy a three-piece suit can create a favorable impression. I wish to dispel this notion up front. In reality, image is more than just a veneer. The idea is *not* to create an illusion or facade but to call attention to real professional capabilities.

Image and Quality

Image sells, quality counts is a theme I've adopted to best express my approach to image building. Without something of value to back it up, image means little. There are proven ways of putting your "quality" to work in the situations that confront you every day, helping you cope with tasks and improving the way you present yourself. A computer sales representative remarks,

> When I'm calling on a potential client, I know that my image gets me in the door. The quality of my product is what they're after, but if I don't have the right image, product quality goes unnoticed.

The same holds true for brand names. When you buy aspirin, for example, you're likely to buy a brand name. Why? Package recognition. Product image. You respect the brand name and its reputation for quality, but recognizing the package motivates you to buy. The image of the product may account for short-term success, but it also helps to establish the long-term reputation of quality. Carry this idea over to the image of successful corporations. Initially, their image helps them gain recognition for a short term. But the quality of their product or service establishes their long-term image.

Advertising and marketing experts carefully design marketing strategy so that the package catches your attention and prompts you to buy. Their strategy takes advantage of mental cues, some subtle, others not so subtle: the unique shape and design of the package, the color, and the labeling, for example. These cues make the product stand out from other products and motivate consumers to buy.

You can gain, or you possess and can polish, some of the same cues, subtleties of body shape, of color and design in clothes, of body posture and movement, of voice, of attitude. You can put these subtleties to work so that your image stands out. Incorporating these signals into your behavior increases your professional credibility and standing.

A question running through your mind might be, "How can my image help me succeed?" Projecting a professional image alone does not guarantee success. Look at your image as an aid for achieving success, a way of establishing a "beachhead."

Success begins with looking and acting successful; it pays to look and act like a winner. A lobbyist for a national drug firm drove the point home in describing the value of image to her success:

> I paid little attention to image when I first started my job. Only when I realized that my job is about 80 percent image—how I present myself—did my effectiveness increase and my superiors take note of me.

Improving your image increases your chances for career growth. How? First, those who control your career growth will recognize your concern for doing the best job. Second, improved style increases effective communication in your job. You make a more convincing overall impression on business peers and superiors, improving personnel relations. Finally, awareness of the image expected in your profession and by your corporation reflects professional competence and dedication.

Many people feel that hard work and doing a good job gain them recognition. This simply is not always the case. Conveying easily recognized, dynamic impressions is often the key that unlocks the door to success—getting the job, winning the promotion, increasing the sales profit. Whether you begin a career, climb the ladder in a

Fortune 500 company, or build your own business, a solid, believable image can help you reach your ultimate career goals.

In short, your image is a tool for communicating and for revealing your inherent qualities, your competence, abilities and leadership. It is a reflection of qualities that others associate with you, a reflection that bears long-lasting influence in your bid for success. Image is not a tool for manipulation. Nor is it a false front. It cannot substitute for substance.

The First Impression

Some people dismiss the impact of first impressions: "It's only an impression, it couldn't be that important." On the contrary. It's been said that in the business and professional world, people form their lasting impression of you within 30 seconds of meeting you. The consequence of a job interview is the best example of the seriousness of the first impression. Career counselors repeatedly state that the first impression made by a job seeker determines whether the applicant is hired. One Washington-based counselor estimates that she decides within the first five or ten minutes whether the prospect is right for the job.

As an icebreaker, and to prove the validity of first impressions, participants in the seminars I lead play an image perception game. This activity proves that the first impression matters. Participants pair off, strangers. Without talking to each other, they write out short descriptions of their partners based on their brief perceptions. They make guesses about personality—about authoritativeness, extroversion or introversion, and profession. After writing the descriptions, the partners exchange them. Each person judges how close his partner's description is to his true self. As a general rule, the estimates are fairly accurate. Although seminar members become better acquainted as the seminar progresses, they admit that the first impressions they form stick.

Research substantiates the fact that impressions, the first impression in particular, stick. One study [1] verifies a "primary effect" information presented *first* is most *decisive*. The first impression is critical because it serves as a foundation for building later opinions. Another study concludes that we have a "tendency to extend a favorable impression of one trait to other traits." [2] If we first see a person in a favorable light, we are likely to continue to make favorable associations with that person.

Turn this thinking around. If others first perceive you in a favorable light, they're likely to continue to do so. Because this initial contact is so important, many companies go to great lengths to insure that employees present a pleasant one. One national car rental agency guarantees that the telephone will be answered within three rings and by a pleasant, helpful voice. Another company trains each new employee in appropriate telephone manners.

These companies have learned that the voice answering the telephone is often the first image a client receives, and that this first impression influences the potential client either to do business or to go elsewhere. The first contact indicates to a client the way the organization operates. If phone service is slow or disagreeable, the client will conclude that business with the company will likely also be slow and disagreeable: "I want no part of that company." The impression you create, the image you project, may well be the determining factor that others use in deciding to do business with you.

Refocusing

Andy is a rising executive in a large state bank. He joined the bank immediately after college, and now he is married and a recent father. When he first started work at the bank he was tagged with the nickname "Junior." As he began to move in higher circles, he

[1] *Carl I. Hovland,* The Order of Presentation in Persuasion, *Vol. I (New Haven: Yale University Press, 1957).*
[2] *Stewart L. Tubbs and Sylvia Moss,* Human Communication *(New York: Random House, 1977).*

wanted to be rid of the junior executive image. To rid himself of the image as Junior, he found he had to drop some of his previous associates and move in more respected and conservative circles. His style gradually erased the less serious image.

Like Andy, most of my clients and seminar participants express a need to change their images. Some clients seem to feel that a new suit or hair style guarantees a changed image. Small surface changes may prove a temporary shot in the arm, but a serious change usually produces serious consequences. Sudden, drastic change in image should be avoided. Marketing expert Otto Kleppner makes a point about changing the image of a product that is useful for the professional or business person:

> When a package is to be changed, it is often done on a gradual basis, changing only one element at a time, so that old customers will not suddenly feel that this is no longer the product they have known and trusted.[3]

Similarly, most business environments are conservative and distrust drastic change. Business people especially tend to accept new ideas only gradually, one at a time. Another reason for the gradual approach is to allow time to test the change. We play a variety of roles in life, and some of them demand different images. With the gradual approach, if you feel uncomfortable with an image or find it doesn't fit the circumstances, you stand a better chance of adjusting it easily.

Refocusing an image depends in large measure on professional demands. If you, like Andy, work in a conservative profession, a noticeable change in appearance or an overactive concern for high-level policy making may raise an eyebrow or two. The attempted change might backfire.

Before drastically refocusing your image, give some consideration to personal and professional needs. A changed image may de-

---

[3] Otto Kleppner, Advertising Procedure (Englewood Cliffs, N.J.: Prentice Hall, 1973).

pend on a changing life style. If your job includes only social and business contacts within the town where you live and work, the type of image you're expected to project is much different from that of someone who travels around the globe. If you move into a job that demands more authority, creating a more authoritative image may be your objective. If you change jobs, moving from an academic to a sales career, for example, you may find that a more persuasive and dynamic image is needed.

As you think about refocusing, keep the following guidelines in mind. You may wish to write out answers and keep a running record of your needs as they change.

1. Define your immediate goals. Do you want a new job or promotion? If you're climbing the ladder in a large corporation, observe and study the image of top-level executives. If all you want is to expand your circle of friends you may need a warmer, more approachable style.

2. What is your single biggest image problem? Is this a major problem or only a minor one?

3. Describe the image you would like to have. Does your life style now demand a more glamorous image? Are you in the public eye? Must you convey an image with greater public visibility?

4. To get a feel for the type of image you should project, consider the five most important people you deal with on a regular basis, both socially and in business. What are their images like? Does your image imitate what they project?

5. To discover your present image, make and keep an image cue list. People send cues about your image by the roles they expect you to play. Listen to others for these cues. How do other people refer to you? Are you referred to as brotherly, sisterly, an adviser, a chum, or the chief cook and bottle washer? Do subordinates usually agree or disagree with you? Do you give advice or demand solutions? If others recognize and respect your ideas, very likely you are expressing a healthy image. If not, a change in attitude may be in order.

6. Another means for discovering your present image is to ask someone close to you—your spouse or a close friend—to describe you. Compare that description with your picture of yourself.

7. Study your physical image. Stand in front of a mirror and take yourself apart. Write out a physical description. What does the total picture look like?

8. Verbalize your present image, but state it in the past tense. This puts you on the way to getting rid of the old image. Then state your preferred image in the present tense. This helps you to see yourself differently.

9. Keep in mind that there is no right or wrong image but that image must change to meet changing circumstances. Your social image is quite different from the image you present to your boss and peers. Gauge the situation and plan your image accordingly.

The Competitive Edge

The professional looking for success in today's business world faces previously uncharted trends. Double-digit inflation, high unemployment rates, and the entry of thousands of well-qualified men and women into the career market are only a few of the influences shaping today's tight job market. Moreover, computers and other technological innovations continue to render many jobs obsolete.

Today's professional must find an edge for winning. Under mounting pressure to compete and succeed, thousands feel lost. Yet many do compete and win.

With greater frequency, losers are asking themselves, "I have qualifications almost identical to those of winners. Why am I not getting ahead?" Or, "I have the credentials for promotion—a good education, solid career experience, an excellent record on this job—why don't I get the promotion?" One major observable difference divides the losers and the winners: the winners project a strong, confident, and persuasive image.

Image
in the World Around You

Image is a major part of the new American reality. We are surrounded by images, from status symbols like fur coats, yachts, and initials on license plates to images projected by the media—television, radio, movies, magazines, newspapers, telephones, and now home video. The society we're living in, more than any prior to it, is a product of media and the impressions they communicate. Television and film have made today's society largely visual.

The importance of image is not new. A brief chronology of image in earlier societies illustrates its relevance. In the Bible God creates man in His own image. Literature, art, philosophy, and religion have always expressed themes in images and image contrasts. Humans have always been fascinated by their ability to draw and preserve pictures of their life styles. Earliest peoples etched spectacular images on cave walls. As civilizations emerged, people continued to express details of their world. Figures of gods, conquests, daily life, and rituals were struck on massive stone pyramids and temples. Wood, gold, silver, bronze, clay and bone were their media.

Although centuries have passed, people are still fascinated with relaying information about their world through images in media.

Only the media have changed. Now print, produced by the printing press, and broadcast, produced by electronic technology, allow communication around the globe.

Inside and outside of business, creation and communication of image play a vital role in reflecting and shaping our cultural attitudes. It's almost impossible to pick up a newspaper or magazine without finding an article projecting someone's image. Modern political candidates realize that winning elections depends on the image they project. Movie and television stars win popularity and fashion pop culture with images modeled on audience fantasies. The executive woman questions and redefines her image as she moves into the previously male dominated business world. Corporate involvement in national and international policymaking requires corporations to bring their image under close scrutiny.

Image is a dynamic force around you. The image of the politician, of executive women, and of the corporation are only three of the images that reflect and shape our culture. These three topics are discussed because they go to the heart of the increasing role of image in our culture.

Image and Politics

What voters see in a candidate depends upon what the candidate deliberately conveys in his speeches, radio and television appearances, political advertising, personal contacts, etc.[1]

"Reagan Wins: Candidate's Image a Determining Factor in Debate." This was the conclusion of an opinion poll conducted in one of my classes in nonverbal communication. As Joe McGinnis points out, candidates deliberately convey an image to voters. Image now plays a major role in deciding a winner. Voters turn to the candidates' images, especially the debate style, to judge the candidates and their stands on issues.

[1] *Joe McGinnis,* The Selling of the President 1968 (*New York: Trident Press, 1968*).

Nothing better illustrates image outside the corporation than the marriage of media and image in the campaigns of political aspirants. Media have invaded the political arena in the last 20 years. Television especially has virtually changed the election process. As Tom Shales of *The Washington Post* writes, "It's too late to cry havoc. Television is such an integral part of the political process that some day it may in fact be the political process." [2]

Packaging a candidate or creating for television an image that wins votes may well be the beginning of a new political reality. Image on television first gained serious attention in the 1960 televised debate between Richard Nixon and John Kennedy. That debate is one of the most studied media events in history.

Perceptions of the two candidates by the viewing audience show that image alone gave Kennedy the edge. Kennedy appeared stronger, more active, more colorful, more relaxed, calmer, and more experienced. He looked taller and more muscular, more dynamic and vigorous. As he debated, an open, erect posture, hand gestures, and note taking greatly enhanced him as more concerned and responsive. The viewing audience perceived in Kennedy's image a more youthful, active and persuasive man.

Nixon rated weaker, more passive and tense. Consequently, he seemed less experienced and knowledgeable. Nixon looked slightly shorter, more tired and thinner. He leaned occasionally, stood on one leg from time to time and held onto the podium when speaking.

Mentioned more frequently than any other factor in Nixon's loss was his inability to control an unpleasant facial image—a dark beard, circles under the eyes, a jowly look with downturned lips. Nixon's clothing, a more loosely fitting suit, added to his unkempt image.

Those who listened to the debate on the radio determined Nixon the winner. He was considered by the experts a more experienced debater, addressing issues more specifically. It's possible that Nixon's poor television image deadened his effectiveness and cost him the election.

[2] The Washington Post, *February 24, 1980.*

Since the 1960 debate, image making and political campaigning are inseparable. According to one government report, of the $50 million that each party candidate allocated to the 1980 election, a sizable sum was earmarked for building the candidate's image.

The 1980 debate produced a contrast similar to that of the 1960 debate. Carter, at times attacking Reagan's character, was perceived as more negative. As always, he fought an inability to coordinate pauses and emphases. For example, he paused in midsentence, sometimes interjecting a smile into a very serious statement. This characteristic reflects uncertainty. Carter's southern drawl displeased many. Finally, he appeared tense and defensive, reflecting a lack of confidence.

Mentioned more than any other factor in Reagan's high score was his ability to appear unoffended by Carter's verbal jibes. He took in stride even Carter's comments on his age. Perhaps his training in film helped. In any case, Reagan was definitely seen as more presidential—more sincere, more relaxed, overall stronger. Despite his lack of youth Reagan made a more commanding, active presence. His gestures, though minimal, were precise. At intervals, he turned toward Carter. He smiled more readily and naturally. Several camera angles showed Reagan's height and the depth of his shoulders, both tremendous advantages in the picture that the viewing audience saw.

Building a candidate's image takes more work than meets the eye when you turn on the TV set. Political image making is based not only on the characters of the contenders, but also on sound, proven measures of public expectations. A leading authority on political image making is Dan Nimmo of the University of Tennessee. His book *Popular Images of Politics* provides some of the most comprehensive and scientific knowledge available on political image.

At its simplest, political image making looks at the relationship between the voting public and the candidate seeking election. The electorate usually hold a preconceived idea of what they want in a candidate. The candidate learns what the public wants by turning to public opinion polling organizations, by reading leading national newspapers and magazines, and by watching newscasts. The candidate then adjusts his or her image and campaign to fit the preconceived idea. The ideal image reflects what the public wants. Nimmo has described how voters relate to the candidate:

> People respond to the leader by identifying with him (either loving or hating him) and imitating him. Through symbolic ways leaders persuade people to follow them by identifying with the images these same people have of an "ideal" president, congressman, senator, mayor or other public official.[3]

Voters want to relate to the candidate, and they are likely to seek out qualities in the candidate that reflect their own aspirations and desires. The political candidate's image is judged also by perceived leadership ability, knowledge of voters' problems, and degree of sincerity and trustworthiness. A fatherly image is often sought in potential leaders, perhaps because the voters associate the father with security.

In forming a new image, Nimmo continues, the balancing of voters' expectations and the candidate's previous image is delicate:

> The formation of images of candidates is a subtle transaction between the symbols candidates project to demonstrate their capacity to govern, on the one hand, and the images voters use to evaluate candidates, on the other.

One thing is certain: the candidate's new image has considerable impact upon voting behavior:

> In forming both their long-term and short-term images of politicians, the mass responds to both substantative and stylistic traits of candidates,

[3] Dan Nimmo, Popular Images of Politics: A Taxonomy (Englewood Cliffs, N.J.: Prentice Hall, 1974).

with a tendency to emphasize personal style over political experience; popular images of political leaders are an amalgam of both role and style expectations, and in attempting to build his image no politician can run simply as a government technician or as a popular celebrity.

The image that the successful office seeker projects must reflect more than superficiality, style, or charisma. The urgent call for a presidential debate in the 1980 campaign proved that voters want to observe aspirants in action before they make a voting decision. A debate is a chance for voters to see how the candidates act and handle important campaign issues under pressure. For many, it's their only source of information about the nominees. In the 1980 campaign, for example, it was estimated that as much as 25 percent of the undecided voting public would make a decision based on observations of the Reagan and Carter debate.

Exterior personality must reflect substance. As Nimmo concludes,

> The political candidate who copes successfully, who wins elections, is aware of what he has to offer the voting public just as he is aware of what the public expects. The politician builds his image based upon what he has to offer the voting public—strong background in public service, proven leadership ability, an ability to make sound decisions. He modifies the exterior representation so that voters identify with the substantive, inner image qualifications.

Political image making has evolved into more than superficial packaging. Voters now turn to the candidate's image, particularly the debate image, to judge the candidate and his stand on issues. There is overwhelming evidence that the office seeker's image, especially on television, is a deciding factor in winning an election. The savvy political candidate accepts this fact as a political reality and uses it to best advantage.

Image and Business

Internal Corporate Image

> Sure, we expect our employees to live up to company expectations. Here at the home office we set rather high standards—our executives are very active in local community civic groups. Our national and international sales representatives must also meet the standards we set. We expect them to serve as ambassadors of goodwill.

This statement expresses a typical attitude of senior corporate officers. Corporations and professions do have *image expectations* and they count upon those who work within to meet those expectations.

Think of the names of successful executives you know. Now think of names in the larger corporate world. You remember the names because they're associated with an image of success, personal and corporate. These people are successful because they have sold their substance and established their credibility in the corporate world. In proving themselves, they've risen to positions of satisfaction and great financial rewards. The way they've presented themselves down the line has helped them succeed. As they advanced, dress and manner of presentation, combined with the substance of the image, often won the corporation new business. As a result, they garnered recognition; superiors saw they could handle important jobs, make decisions, and solve problems.

Today's corporate executive may appear at a conference in Geneva on Monday, jet to New York to videotape a public service announcement by Wednesday, and spend the rest of the week in Chicago, attending a stockholders' meeting. The successful corporate executive is groomed to be the type of person who can represent the corporation worldwide if necessary. Looking at someone who looks like the ranks, superiors might think, "We can't have a person like that representing us in Paris."

As corporate executives mature within the company, they take on the responsibility of shaping the image of the entire corporation. The image of one or another chief executive officer may exert global impact.

Within the past decade, the importance of the corporate image transmitted by employees to the outside world, has increased, and it continues to gain momentum. The image of the corporation reflected by employees is called *internal corporate image.* Each person within a company is, in some way, expressing the image of the entire organization. Leonard Silk, an economics columnist for *The New York Times,* and David Vogel, who teaches business administration at the University of California at Berkeley, have explained the broad significance of internal corporate image:

> The importance of a favorable public view of businessmen is not just personal, but economical and political as well. Although the value of public opinion is frequently exaggerated, there can be no question that the degree of congruence between self-image and public image enhances the political strength and legitimacy of business.[4]

Because the need for satisfactory employee image has increased drastically in recent years, corporations are changing to meet the need. They now realize that their reputations may depend on how their employees are viewed by the outside world. For this reason, they use training programs, outside education, participatory management, and profit-sharing plans, among other means, to teach employees how to project an appropriate image.

Because image is so essential, courses and seminars in professional image making, public speaking, video presentation and corporate etiquette have grown in popularity. Burns W. Roper, a pollster who publishes a national series of surveys called the *Roper Reports,* stresses the change in thought:

[4] *Leonard Silk and David Vogel, "Ethics and Profits: The Crisis of Confidence in American Business,"* Saturday Review, *July 10, 1976.*

Business has never placed any particular premium on the qualities that make a person good on television or good on the public stage. One might speculate, however, that in not too many years, most enlightened corporations will make such qualities *high priority job requisites,* for either the chief executive officer or the chief operating officer—or both—and ideally for others in the organization as well. [5]

Employees at every level of the corporation take on job duties that require knowledge of how to come across to others. Their responsibility requires a knowledge not of personal appearance and behavior alone but of the corporation's expectations about appearance and behavior. Many learn the hard way that they are expected to fit a certain mold.

Jim Michaels started as a public service representative for an auto parts manufacturer almost two years ago. A good salary and a liberal company philosophy first attracted him to the job. Jim's main interest in life is music, and his style, though not unkempt or disorganized, is more relaxed than the style of others in the company. When he took the job, he thought that if he just put in a good day's work, he'd be rewarded accordingly. During his first year, he devoted minimal time to company activities, concentrating on music in his spare time.

At the end of the year, he hadn't received a promotion or a raise. At review time, his boss stressed that Jim had shown little interest in the company. Failure to fit the company image had held him back.

Although Jim's company espoused a relatively free style, in reality it expected an image not stated. Those who advanced in the company heeded the unwritten code. As Jim discovered, relaxed dress codes do not mean that hard work alone will necessarily lead to better jobs and pay increases.

Professionals, in or out of the corporation, should fit the image of the work place and the professions they represent. The employee

[5] Public Relations Quarterly, *Summer 1977.*

who is aware of the proper image is more likely to get the top-level job. Those who succeed fit the mold.

Some organizational expectations are easier to detect than others. If you aren't already aware of the image expected in your corporation, take a look around to see what is expected. Observe the style of top-level managers and corporate heads. Ask the opinion of someone you respect and consider successful.

Many corporations specify what they expect in corporate philosophy statements. Some go so far as to spell out dress and behavior codes. Professional associations adhere to a code of ethics. Membership in them requires that you read and obey the rules. Written or unwritten, a very definite image is expected in corporations and professions. Those who move up measure up.

To determine the image expected in their professions, participants in my seminars complete an occupational stereotype exercise. Each person is handed a list of workers in ten to twenty occupations. They range widely, from physician and attorney to custodian and construction worker, from white to blue collar, from high to low salary, and through various education levels. Participants rate each type of worker on perceived prestige, annual income, and average education level. Seminar members write adjectives to describe typical workers in the occupations.

This exercise, which I have repeated dozens of times, always gets similar results. Inevitably, physician and attorney receive the highest prestige rating. Both are members of professions, ranked as white collar, requiring advanced degrees but earning high starting salaries as a reward. Among the terms used to describe a physician are "concerned," "dedicated," and "respected." The attorney is often cast as "untrustworthy," "persuasive," and "aggressive"; he is even called a con artist. Many participants attribute their distrust of the attorney to their association of lawyers with Watergate.

Near the opposite end rank the construction worker and the custodian. Frequently labeled blue collar, the occupations of these workers are rated as less prestigious, requiring less education, and paying a lower starting salary. Terms describing these callings usually include rough, dirty, and masculine.

This exercise demonstrates not only that occupations conjure up prevalent images but that the image of an occupation extends to the entire group of workers within it. The exercise also helps seminar participants begin to define the image expectation in their career. For example, an attorney labeled "untrustworthy" or "aggressive" might well begin to change styles to tone down aggression and build trustworthiness.

Anthony Coxon and Charles Jones, researchers in sociology and joint editors of *Social Mobility,* go a step further:

> A person's profession is the main index of placement in the social and class structure. Since occupation comprises such a large slice of daily life, it influences lifestyle both inside and outside working hours and actually determines social and economic well-being.[6]

To see how much emphasis you place on profession in forming an image of another person, pay close attention to introductions and chatter at the next cocktail party or other social event you attend. Notice the amount of time spent discussing careers and jobs. Signs of income bracket, education level, life style, and level of success are likely the clues that form the picture.

Some occupations are easier to distinguish than others. We know, for example, that a career in fashion or design allows a freer and more creative image than does a career in banking or finance, which demands a more conservative and trustworthy appearance.

External Corporate Image

The familiar face of Bob Hope appears on your television screen decked out in coveralls and hard hat. His message goes something

[6] *Anthony P. M. Coxon and Charles Jones,* The Images of Occupational Prestige *(New York: St. Mary's Press, 1978).*

like this: "Bob Hope here for Texaco. I'd like to tell you what Texaco is doing right now, to guarantee that you get the most for the dollar you spend at the pump." You open the daily paper and read a full-page ad extolling the steps Mobil takes to fight the energy battle. Television spot announcements and newspaper ads are but two of the ways large corporations carve their external corporate image.

External image generally includes any information the corporation wants made known to the public. Creating and maintaining favorable public visibility is a main concern of big business. What the public believes about a corporation determines, in many cases, whether or not the business succeeds. Large oil companies, the insurance industry, airlines, public service and sales organizations, even the federal government, spend millions each year to safeguard their public images.

Small and large corporations alike find that they now do business with numerous audiences, and that they must carefully plan efforts to communicate with all of them. Corporations now play roles that require expertise not only in profit making but in government and foreign relations as well.

The response of tampon manufacturers to the linking of tampons with toxic shock syndrome is a good example of how to deal with public knowledge. Bad publicity and lawsuits in the millions mushroomed into a major problem. Tampon manufacturers responded by warning women to limit their use of tampons. In this way, the manufacturers gained the appearance of responsibility to the public.

Knowing how to influence public opinion and build a favorable environment for business is required of big business if it wants to continue. In a special report to *Business Week,* Loet A. Velmans, president of Hill and Knowlton, the nation's largest public relations firm, warns that corporate survival is increasingly difficult:

The corporation also faces intensified competition in the marketplace, the growing threat of takeover by outsiders, and new challenges in employee relations. And all the while, the corporate community continues to be plagued by a negative public image.[7]

Velmans goes on to say that, in order to survive, corporations are working harder to project a better public image:

> The corporation is being politicized and has assumed another dimension in our society that it did not have as recently as ten years ago. As a result, the corporation has become more conscious of using communications in all its diverse forms as a tool to accomplish its objectives, and it is articulating its position more clearly to government agencies, legislators, shareholders, employees, customers, financial institutions, and other critical audiences.

The weight carried by corporate image was revealed in a study of Wall Street investment decisions. The report discovered that corporate image is far from intangible; it is a big factor in investment selection. Because people are clearly influenced by the corporate image, the analyst must reckon with it too. General Electric's image as "aggressive in product research," or IBM's image of "product and marketing excellence" were cited by the analysts as examples of images that win investors' consideration.

What comprises corporate image? Business management sought opinions on the subject from a cross section of public relations experts, advertising and graphic arts specialists and a fair share of companies. The consensus was that corporate image consists of two different views: one, it's the impression that a corporation tries to convey through advertising, public relations and other means; two, it's the vast number of impressions of the corporation held by a vast array of individuals. These individuals compose publics of different degrees of importance in determining the standing of the corporation.

[7] *Reprinted from* Business Week, *January 22, 1979, by special permission. All rights reserved.*

How does a corporation go about discovering its standing with its publics? Otto Lerbinger at Boston University's School of Public Communication describes one way:

> One kind of specialized corporate survey is a corporate image study. There are at least three types of questions that are typically included: (1) familiarity or awareness questions that determine to what extent, if any, a corporation is known; (2) favorability questions which measure the direction and intensity of how well people like a corporation; and (3) personality traits questions which try to show how the corporation differs in terms of such dimensions as progressiveness, friendliness and profitability.

Lerbinger continues by describing the publics surveyed:

> While the sample for corporate image study may be the general population, it is more frequently limited to specific publics such as local communities, the corporate stockholders, security analysts, employees and opinion leaders.[8]

Shaping and maintaining an image that consumers and other publics believe and trust demands a great deal of sophisticated know-how, dedication, and enthusiasm. Large corporations often have in-house PR departments to shape their images. Others turn to PR firms. But who handles the function or how it's carried out is of lesser importance than the fact that businesses, large and small, are changing the way they think. They now see image as a necessary component of continued success.

Internal and external corporate image come together to send a total picture to those observing the corporation. As a corporate employee, the image you send is a vital part of the total picture.

[8] *Otto Lerbinger,* Designs for Persuasive Communication (*Englewood Cliffs, N.J.: Prentice Hall, 1972). Reprinted by special permission.*

Image and the Professional Career Woman

When Peg separated from her husband she needed to earn a substantial salary immediately. Although she landed a good job with ample pay, she was interested in a promotion as soon as possible. As administrative assistant in a respected brokerage firm, she has worked for a little over a year. Prior to accepting this job, she depended on her husband for economic support as well as social entertainment. Since her divorce, she has had to solve emotional and financial problems as a head of household. She has a daughter and assumes partial responsibility for her support.

Peg falls into a large national category. Census figures show that of some thirty million families with children, six million are single-parent families, headed usually by women. Although she is just a number to statisticians, Peg faces problems which to her are real—competing and succeeding while supporting a family.

Peg wants to be considered for job advancement on the same basis as her colleagues. Yet, she competes with young and very aggressive men and women. The broader scene is of an increasing number of women entering an already crowded job market. Uppermost in the minds of women is economic survival among stiff competition, especially for management jobs. As women flood the job market and climb the corporate ladder, what are the problems they face?

Although women make up 40 percent of the work force, they hold a minority of the responsible, better-paying jobs. Almost 39 million women work, about half of the total female population. Yet, according to recent statistics, 75 percent of them are concentrated in the five predominately "female professions": secretary, stenographer, household worker, bookkeeper, elementary school teacher. Only 5.6 percent hold management or administrative jobs.

The jump from the typical roles as female helper into management is not easy. Part of the difficulty stems from the stereotypes of women held by men in the work world. Part of the problem lies in the image that women hold of themselves. More than half of my clients are women. Consistently they express two problems: one, emerging as independent professionals from the shadow of their husbands' careers, and two, succeeding in their jobs while combating the forces of unfavorable stereotypes.

Many women feel they live in the shadow of their husband's job. They assume the image of the diplomat's wife, the minister's wife, or the wife of the policeman. These women play out the supporting social role dictated by the husband's job rather than create distinct identities for themselves.

The corporate wife is a good example. One corporate wife said that she feels her needs rank lower than those of her husband and children. Her husband's career is of utmost importance; her financial and emotional security derive from his high-level position; his success is the key to her status and contentment; and her sense of accomplishment is in seeing him prosper.

Many women feel they're the victims of their own stereotype of women. In defining and achieving personal success, they battle their own learned social attitudes that competition, professional competence, intellectual achievement, and corporate success are basically inconsistent with femininity.

My observation is that the professional woman is suffering role conflict. The problem is compounded as she begins to succeed. Moving up from a subordinate—"feminine"—position in a male-dominated world, she encounters the bias of "how women should be."

Marian is typical. "I'm fighting both my husband's expectations and the expectations of my company. As a manager, I am being tested by both. I'm really confused as to how I should act."

Some women overreact to the conflict. At one extreme, some project an image of severity and control, especially on the job. Perhaps this is an attempt to compete with male counterparts by being recognized as equally "masculine." At the other extreme, perhaps in an attempt both to attract male peers and to prove themselves, some project a very strong feminine image, an image that says, "I'm a woman, but I can stick with the best of them."

Women want jobs, particularly in management, but confusion about self-presentation is a major drawback. To be taken seriously, women must both know how to handle job problems and display proper qualities.

At first, Marian couldn't understand why she wasn't living up to expectations. The reasons soon became clear. When she sat on the board of directors, she hesitated to take a leading role. She felt the more aggressive, senior men would not take her suggestions seriously. As the only female board member, she thought others saw her as the token minority. Her fear of speaking up held her back from getting recognition.

When she spoke out and made her views known, however, she was taken seriously. She learned to handle the problem in the course of completing an image seminar. She learned to wear darker, more authoritative clothes, to tone down her makeup and jewelry, and to speak confidently. Consequently, she gained the respect and stature she wanted. As a manager and board member she was expected to be a leader. Only when she saw herself as a leader was she taken seriously.

For Marian, the solution was both to learn how to handle business tasks and to become associated with management qualities. To succeed, women must employ the same methods men have used; one such method is projecting the right image.

Nancy Thompson, a Washington-based consultant who works with women, explained to me in a personal interview that women have few models to follow, that they lack a clear understanding of what image is expected. There are very few role models to guide women, very few women with real power. On the other hand, according to Thompson, men are clones. The successful male executive knows what to look like and how to behave to achieve the image that will win power and success.

Women are confused about what constitutes the image of a successful managerial woman. Occupational roles are confused with sex roles, perhaps because most managers are men.

Breaking out of a stereotype is not easy. It takes time and perseverance. The solution to the problem begins with a change in attitude and habits—by both men and women—and a concentration on professional growth. As Nancy Thompson explained, women must start by changing their attitude. They must want to succeed. While recognizing that there are stereotypes, women can realize that they don't exist simply for their husbands. They must be willing to go out on their own, and they must have education, timing, luck, and a sense of humor. "You'll encounter some hard times and run into some brick walls," said Thompson. "Don't get mad or try to get even. Persevere. . . . A stick-with-it attitude is all-important."

When I asked her what single bit of advice she'd give the professional woman who wants to reach the top, Thompson replied: "Put together a career plan. Analyze your assets, find out what you have to offer. Sit down and chart your plan. Set goals, be willing to change plans to meet new goals."

Changing attitude, developing a career strategy, and projecting an assertive image in the job, day to day, are the beginnings for breaking the stereotype. They're also awfully big tasks for anyone.

Part II

ENHANCEMENT OF PERSONAL IMAGE
Focus on the Individual

Self-Image:
A Solid Interior

"Know thyself," said Socrates, and this wisdom is inscribed over the entrance to the Temple of Apollo at Delphi.

A healthy self-image is the base for a healthy professional attitude. Each of us carries around with us a mental blueprint of ourselves that expresses itself to others in the way we carry out duties, handle others, and reach decisions on the job. Maxwell Maltz, a renowned plastic surgeon who has studied physical and psychological adjustment, writes, "the self-image is a premise, a base, or a foundation upon which your entire personality, your behavior, and even your circumstances are built." He continues:

> When the self-image is intact and secure, you feel good. When it is threatened, you feel anxious and insecure. When it is adequate and one that you can be wholeheartedly proud of, you feel free to be yourself and to express yourself. You function at your optimum.[1]

How important is the self-image to success?

Zig Ziglar, author of *See You at the Top,* states unequivocally that "the starting point for both success and happiness is a healthy

[1] *Maxwell Maltz,* Psycho-Cybernetics (*Englewood Cliffs, N.J.: Prentice Hall, 1960*).

self-image." He explains that a poor self-image manifests itself in poor physical appearance and bearing.

> Such people often dress unattractively, forego personal hygiene, frequently become obese, abandon morality and flaunt immorality, turn to drugs or alcohol and become vulgar and profane in speech. It's distressing to see sloppy, dirty, profane and unkempt individuals because the outward appearance is a dead giveaway to the self-image.[2]

An unhealthy self-image is destructive. It affects what we express to the outside world and our ability to succeed.

The influence of the self-image is illustrated by a client who first contacted me during his search for a new job. During interviews, he felt at the mercy of the company interviewing him; he felt he was asking a favor of the prospective employer. His nervousness and poor self-image became so pervasive that interviewers couldn't ignore it.

My first advice was that he needed to change his attitude toward himself, to think of himself this way: "I am me, I have valuable credentials to offer. I can be a real asset to your company." His attitude changed from wondering what the company could do for him to knowing what he had to offer the company. As soon as his attitude shifted, he interviewed with a relaxed air, projecting a self-confident image.

Maltz states the secret to discovering the healthy self-image:

The secret is this: to really "live," that is to find life reasonably satisfying, you must have an adequate and realistic self-image that you can live with. You must find your self acceptable to "you." You must have a wholesome self-esteem. You must have a self that you are not ashamed to "be" and one that you can feel free to express creatively, rather than to hide or cover up. You must have a self that corresponds to reality so that you can function effectively in a real world. You must know yourself, both your strengths and weaknesses and be honest with yourself

[2] Zig Ziglar, See You at the Top (Gretna, La.: Pelican Publishing, 1975).

concerning both. Your self-image must be a reasonable appoximation of "you," being neither more than you are, nor less than you are.

Building the Self-Image

If a positive self-image is so important, how do we go about building it? Dr. G. Othell Hand, Vice President of Motivation for American Family Life Assurance Company, told me in a personal interview that self-image can be built through strategic involvement, by being "carried away by a sense of meaning and significance, whether one's role is near the bottom or at the top of the corporate ladder."

Howard Newberger and Marjorie Lee perhaps best sum up the construction of a positive self-image:

> A flexible structure, it possesses the potential for expansion. It can be compared with a house, constructed in such a way that other rooms can be added without demolishing the original core. To a much greater degree than has been realized, we are able to affect and reaffect the way in which we view ourselves. Self-image modification is a step by step process toward success in terms of individual wishes and expectations. The choice of direction is ours.[3]

Building a positive self-image requires a knowledge of what this core consists of and adoption of the qualities associated with the professional that are lacking. Having understood the way we view ourselves, we can modify this first self-image to better handle the problems we run up against.

Modifying the self-image requires a willingness to change and to go through some self-examination. For many, this is frightening. Yet, discovering the self can be the most fascinating aspect of being alive. Changing or developing self-image is not so much a process of changing as it is of actualizing what you want and already have the

[3] *Howard M. Newberger and Marjorie Lee,* Winners and Losers: The Art of Self-Image Modification (*New York: David McKay, 1974*).

potential to become. It's not a static process but a continuing one. The blueprint of self must be updated to match new experiences and growth. Self-actualization is magical, the chance to grow into what you want to be. Look at discovery of self-image this way: It's like a long-awaited vacation. Each new place you visit provides the impetus for a thrilling new adventure. You can hardly wait to reach the next spot on your itinerary.

To help discover the qualities of a healthy self-image, I poll participants in my seminars, professionals themselves, to find out what they consider important. Repeatedly, the qualities that rated highest: self-confidence, expertise, responsibility, and motivation.

Self-Confidence

People are just naturally attracted to a self-confident person. Confidence, rated the number one quality respected in a professional, is an attitude of certainty. Degree of self-confidence varies from person to person. Since each person is shaped by different influences, no two people are exactly alike, not even identical twins. One twin may grow up to be very confident while the other may lack confidence. Dr. Clara Mayo of Boston University states:

> Confidence is not genetic—like blond hair or blue eyes. It is yours for developing. It comes with age, life experiences and interaction with family, friends, teachers and work associates. In the formative years, parents bear the burden of sending you down the road of self-esteem. Parents succeed only if they make a deliberate effort to put you in situations where you face decisions.[4]

The process of making decisions and living with them builds a feeling of worth that carries over into the rest of a lifetime.

[4] The Washington Post, *October 29, 1979.*

Self-confidence can be built at any age and begins with a willingness for some healthy self-examination. You want to discover your special abilities and skills. Begin by deciding what type of person you consider yourself to be. Ask yourself, what sets you apart? What makes you stand out from the crowd? Make a list of your strengths. Take time to examine and list special skills, the ability to manage people, for example. Praise yourself. Keep this list handy and, when you're feeling low or insecure, refer back to it for reassurance and encouragement. The list will give you a positive perspective on yourself. Identifying your unique set of abilities and strengths will contribute to your feelings of worth and pride.

Similarly, list your weaknesses. To recognize a problem is the first step toward resolving it. Study your weaknesses to determine how you can overcome them and build strengths. A weakness may simply be a habit that's holding you back. For example, if lack of assertiveness is a problem, simply deciding to state your opinion in a meeting is a first step. You may need outside help to break a habit. Often a close friend or spouse is willing to help you work on this. Get to the roots of personal inadequacies so you can turn them around. For example, if you discover that the lack of a course in human relations is keeping you from a promotion, consider enrolling in a night course. This kind of honest self-examination will reward you in the long run by leading to image-building solutions to problems.

Developing self-confidence requires that you know that you're unique, that you have strengths and weaknesses and that you are a person who can command respect. Another exercise many use to help discover and build self-confidence is writing out a life story. They include in the story the times they felt most proud, the times they were happiest and the times they felt they were achieving. You may want to do the same thing. Writing out your story is time consuming, but referring to it and responding to it as you grow will reinforce your sense of pride and confidence. You will feel that you're in control of your life and making progress toward achieving the success you want.

Expertise

Closely allied to a sense of self-confidence is the feeling that you're capable of doing a good job. Expertise is built on the experiences that enable you to meet the demands of your career—education, job training, job experience, and other valuable life and career accomplishments. Continued expertise requires keeping up with career and corporate trends and developments.

Expertise also includes high ethical standards. All professions and corporations have ethical standards, and members are expected to live up to them.

How do you build expertise? In writing your life story or listing your strengths, emphasize all your valuable life experiences rather than career experiences alone. Include, that is, not only education and special training, but also hobbies, talents, and personal achievements.

Take another look at your career and the corporation you work for. What are their requirements? Do you need additional training and education to become an expert? Should you read additional professional journals to keep abreast of new career trends? Talk to successful work associates to find out the standards they adhere to. To grow in your career, you may need to enroll in a night course or get additional training.

Responsibility

Responsibility is the dedication to doing a good job. Whether you're leading a *Fortune* 500 company or working in an assembly line, responsibility means you take pride in doing a good job. Corporations respect and promote those who take their career growth in hand. The person with a healthy self-image accepts the responsibility for personal development and nurtures the ability to study job problems and come up with plans for resolving them.

A sense of responsibility is learned in childhood. Responsibility and self-confidence seem to develop hand in hand as children grow, provided that parents place them in situations that require them to make decisions—managing an allowance, for example. Again, early development of a sense of duty carries over and helps them manage their life and career.

When I interviewed Dr. G. Othell Hand, I asked him about the corporate executive and responsibility. He responded that responsibility is nothing short of reliability, so that the question becomes, "can you be depended on?" A dependable corporate employee will, when faced with a difficult problem, consider these guidelines:

1. Develop an overview of the total problem or situation. Sum it up to determine who is involved and what the heart of the problem is. How does the problem affect the entire organization and the individuals directly involved?

2. What are the alternatives? List them. A logical question to ask yourself about each one: "If I handle the situation this way, what are the likely outcomes?"

3. Consider the suggestions of others. Effective managers listen. There is little room for the attitude that "mine is the only way."

4. Reach a decision. Base your decision on solutions to similar problems. Call on the experience of others, if needed.

5. Decide on a procedure to implement the decision. Who should handle what? What time frame are you talking about? What are the monetary considerations?

6. Develop a system for follow-up. Check to see whether what you have implemented works or whether it should be revised to meet changing needs.

Responsible people control their personal development as well as their career growth. They care enough about their own welfare to define what they expect from life, and they work hard to achieve what they want.

A clear definition of success is the first step. Marilyn is a good example of the many people who have difficulty in defining personal success. Out of college for three years, she works as a salesagent for a hotel chain. She likes the job and her boss. Dedicated to her work, she's received two promotions and substantial salary increases. Yet, on occasion, she feels she isn't really getting anywhere.

When asked how she defines success and whether she has set goals for reaching that success, she seems almost startled. Her response: "I really hadn't given that much thought." Marilyn is typical of people so wrapped up in the expectations of their corporation that their personal growth suffers. Working within corporate expectations is most important, but giving some thought to personal goals is also important. Corporations ordinarily respect those who accept responsibility for planning their careers, and for intertwining personal and corporate expectations. The result is a more productive employee who avoids an unnecessary and perhaps unwanted dependency upon the employer.

Like Marilyn, you might not have thought about where you're headed. Maybe you're too involved in your job. We tend not to block out much time for planning our lives, yet we're disappointed when things don't satisfy us.

Regardless of age or the success you've already achieved, setting goals is the only means for getting what you want out of the rest of life. The ability to set goals and reach them strengthens the self-image by reinforcing the image of responsibility. In essence, you are saying, "I'm in control of my life. I know where I'm headed."

If you haven't made a life or career plan or revised one lately, raise the curtain by planning where you want to be ten years from now. List long-term goals and then list what you want to accomplish within shorter time frames—in five years, in one year, in six months. Let these short-term goals support the long-term goal. Make your plan realistic, but set goals high enough to challenge you. Check off each goal as you reach it, and then move on to the next one. Start your plan right now.

To get an idea of the importance of goal setting and career planning, look at this time frame: The average life span is 70 years. Career span is less, usually starting around age 18 to 20 and ending at about age 62 to 65. This means that in a typical lifetime, approximately 40 to 45 years are spent working.

To gain a perspective, draw a straight line to represent the life line:

0 years	70 years
Birth	Death

Place a check mark on the point that represents your current age. How much of your life has already passed? How much is left?

Do the same for career:

18–20 Years	60–65 years
Career Begins	Retirement

Place a check mark on the point of your present career. How much time do you have left?

Developing a clear-cut set of attainable goals and reaching them produces a visible change in your self-image. Others see you differently—as determined to get to where you want to go and able to get there. You appear more confident and reliable, in greater control of your life.

Motivation

Questions that might be running through your mind: "Is this as easy as it looks? Once goals and a career plan are set, how can I be assured that I'll be motivated?"

Again and again, success hinges on staying motivated. Even with goals and an organized career plan, an unmotivated person is not likely to succeed.

Motivation is the desire to act in order to reach goals. When I asked Dr. Hand to suggest a prescription for building motivation, he replied,

> Motivation is the key, the spark of life within us that can be fanned into flame by exciting goals, satisfying performance, rewarding achievement. It is an inner process which fuels itself, once we have begun with the initial step of personal goal setting.

Motivated and successful people often describe motivation and goal attainment as a circular process. Reaching one goal provides the needed boost for reaching the next goal. Admittedly, events in life cannot always be planned or controlled, but their negative effects can be minimized if you hold in front of you the benefits you'll derive from reaching your goals.

Paul J. Meyer, president of the Success Motivation Institute International, Inc., offers a five-step formula that has helped many remain motivated.

1. Crystallize your thinking. Set a definite goal with a definite time limit for its achievement. Nebulous generalities such as "wealthy by middle age" will not suffice. Set a goal of an exact salary by a certain date.

2. Make a concrete plan for attaining your goal. Write it down.

3. Develop a burning desire to reach your goals. Make an exhaustive list of every possible benefit to be derived from reaching your goal.

4. Maintain unshakable faith in your ability to accomplish your purpose. Make a study of one person, or several people, who have already achieved success. Note in particular the qualities that have made them successful. List their qualities and compare the list with your own.

5. Create a force of iron-willed determination that will blast all obstacles from your path. If the benefits to be derived from achieving your goal are worthwhile, any person or situation in the way will be a thief, stealing from your future success. Make your determination so strong that it will eliminate any situation or circumstance between you and your goal.[5]

Dr. Hand stresses the importance to motivation of developing and maintaining a healthy self-image:

> The people who make their mark in the world have one trait in common—they believe in themselves. Despite all preachments to the

[5] "Self-Motivation," Inspection News, May 1966.

contrary, self-esteem is an emotion to be nourished and utilized. Moralists often wield the word "selfish" like a bludgeon, cracking down on all forms of self-consideration until sensitive beings are persuaded that whatever is to one's advantage is forbidden. But the English playwright Shakespeare was not one of those moralists; declared he: "Self love, my liege, is not so vile a sin as self neglecting."

The best medicine for an unhealthy self-image is prevention. Remaining confident and motivated is the essence of a healthy self-image. Outside pressures sometimes seem overpowering. The following list of guidelines has proved valuable to many others in times when the self-image is bruised. Keep it and refer to it often.

1. Develop an attitude that says, without boasting, "I can because I am—I am a creature of God, divinely endowed to master the circumstances that surround me."

2. Overcome feelings of inferiority. Learn to think and feel that you're important, that you're the single most important person alive. It's from you that all else begins. You create your own reality. There are billions of people alive today, but there is only one *you*. You are extremely valuable; you have an original set of talents just waiting to be used. If you're not using them, what are you waiting for?

3. Use your mind. You are blessed with a brain that can create thoughts in seconds. Science has never reconstructed any apparatus that duplicates the brain. The waste of a human mind is the greatest waste known to mankind. Successful people use their minds.

4. Put away feelings of unhappiness and worthlessness. Just looking at another person, you sense his feeling of self-acceptance or self-rejection. A content person shows it through happiness and through friendliness toward others. When you feel good about yourself you automatically put others at ease.

5. Beware of people with whom you associate. If you're around people who are negative and depressed, who have low morale, you will soon absorb these feelings. Learn to associate with people who are optimistic and enthusiastic about life and you will soon pick up their optimism. Life is short; make the most of it.

6. Avoid being totally self-centered. Do something for someone else. The satisfaction you gain goes beyond just helping out another person. The ability to help someone creates a feeling within you that you are fortunate. A trait of successful people is that they enjoy helping others.

7. Learn to relate comfortably to success. Defining and winning success seems to many such a monumental task that they tend to shy away from it. Most simply will not accept the responsibility that goes along with success. This innate fear of success hinders the very process. Once you step out of this mold and accept responsibility for what you can do, you have taken the first giant step forward.

8. Personal appearance shows that you care. Although outward appearance cannot substitute for assets, a sharp personal appearance makes you feel good. A change in outward appearance is often the beginning of a change in inner image. Outward appearance can enhance or cripple the potential of the person hiding inside.

Status and Stature: Success Begins with Body Size and the Way You Dress

Suppose someone told you that if you're over six feet tall, you have a better chance of making a million dollars or ending up as chairman of the board. Would you believe that? Height alone does not guarantee a high salary or a top-level job, but evidence suggests that your height, weight, and body shape and size can be an advantage or a disadvantage as you climb the ladder. If you're overly tall, you may be intimidating others by your height. If you're short, your lack of height may be signaling a lack of clout.

Do People Really React to Our Bodies?

Using physical image for optimum impact demands an awareness of what your shape, size, and stature are communicating. Body types—large, small, thin, hefty—contain built-in image problems. These problems can be minimized by the slight change of wearing clothing that enhances your natural endowments.

Michelle Barron is a case in point. She has just realized a lifelong ambition. With her children grown and away from home, she recently started a small business as an organization consultant. She put her experience as an office assistant and her training in interior design to work by planning and arranging small businesses, often helping small business owners set up their offices.

Michelle is over six feet tall and is considered stocky due to a naturally large bone structure. The dark suits she wore, her short, severe hair style, and her large-framed glasses added to her intimidating image. Her height and weight, combined with severe, authoritative clothes, made her look domineering to her clients.

Michelle made her appearance more relaxed and less dominating by exchanging the glasses for contacts and by wearing lighter, less authoritative dresses to deemphasize her build and low-heeled shoes to decrease her height. Now, to decrease the dominating impact of her size, when she meets clients she arranges to seat herself with them around an informal table rather than alone behind a large desk. Not only does she feel more comfortable but her client list is starting to grow. The informal seating arrangement and less intimidating wardrobe make her clients feel more at ease.

The body is a primary tool we use to communicate and respond to other people. Bodies possess great power and force; they convey strength or weakness, superiority or inferiority, attractiveness or unattractiveness, and authority or lack of it. Bodies measure movement through time and space; they exert force through weight and bulk. Through our bodies we learn to experience pain and joy; we feel good, become ill, know youth, and grow old. Through them we also signal our intent to others.

Stereotypes about physical attractiveness are determinant factors in our response to others and their response to us. Studies of attractiveness and persuasiveness show, for example, that audiences react more favorably to an attractive speaker. Attractive persons, regardless of sex, achieve credibility easily.

Mark L. Knapp of Purdue University expands the idea that we hold preconceived ideas about body types:

We have been trained for so long to believe that stereotypes are harmful distortions of the truth, we often fail to consider another equally plausible explanation—that a particular stereotype may be the result of a distillation of ages of social experience. In other words, a stereotype may be more accurate than we wish to admit—there may be some reason for the stereotypes other than prejudicial whims. Clearly, the evidence shows that we do associate certain personality and temperament traits with certain body builds. These expectations may or may not be accurate, but they do exist; they are a part of the psychological mortar in interpersonal communication. We must recognize these stereotypes as potential stimuli for communication responses so we can deal with them more effectively.[1]

If a case can be made that there are clearly defined and generally accepted physique–temperament stereotypes, we can reason that our body types have a lot to do with the way people perceive and respond to us.

If we judge others by body type, we judge them more by the clothes they wear. When we encounter people on the street, at lunch, or after work over cocktails, we guess what their jobs might be by the way they dress. We categorize entire groups of workers by the uniforms they choose—policemen, nurses, waiters, and mail carriers. We categorize blue-collar and white-collar careers and make assumptions about education level, status, and income. We may go so far as to match a personality to the profession, basing our guess entirely on the way a person dresses.

Professions appear to have their own expectations regarding the dress of employees. Jobs with higher public visibility demand a better dressed person than jobs with little or no public contact. Indeed, people may choose professions that encourage them to express their individuality. Contrast Earl, a buyer with a large department store, to John, an accountant in a small firm. As a buyer, Earl has learned a

---

[1] *Mark L. Knapp,* Nonverbal Communication in Human Interaction *(New York: Holt, Rinehart and Winston, 1972). Reprinted by permission.*

great deal about how to dress; he chooses fabrics, colors, and styles that complement his personality. He wears fashionable but tasteful suits with colorful accessories. Considered an extrovert and sociable, on and off the job, he's well liked by the other buyers and his clients.

By contrast, John sticks to himself. He dresses well but conservatively, usually in gray or dark three-piece suits. His conservative nature limits his contact with others in the office as well as with the public. His social life centers around small cocktail parties and dinner dates.

Certain styles do indeed go with certain professions. In this case, a freer, more expressive style goes with the career in fashion, while the more conservative, less flamboyant style fits a career in finance.

The clothes you wear can enhance or detract from your effectiveness as you go about your job. They should suit the style of your profession. Dressing in a dark suit certainly imparts a more authoritative, high-status image than wearing blue jeans or a leisure suit. Meeting a potential client when you are dressed in less authoritative clothes may cost you the contract. Subordinates are less likely to take seriously a manager or supervisor who shows up every day at the office in designer jeans and an open shirt. Reporting to the board of directors may provoke a sneer if you dress in disco fashion with flashy jewelry.

There's not much we can do to grow another six inches, and it may take months to lose 50 pounds, but we can minimize our problems and elicit better responses through choosing the right clothes. Your body type may be a problem, but your clothes can alleviate it.

Body Types, and How to Make the Most of What You Have

For convenience, researchers have divided body types into three groups: endomorph, mesomorph, and ectomorph. The endomorph is soft, round, and fat and is referred to as the hefty type. The mesomorph is muscular and athletic and is referred to as the muscular or tall ideal. The ectomorph is also tall but appears thin and fragile, and is referred to as the thin type. For the purposes of this book I've added a category, the small or short person.

Wells and Siegel performed an interesting study that shows we have stereotyped body types.[2] They showed silhouette drawings of the endomorph, mesomorph, and ectomorph to 120 adults and asked them to rate the types on 24 scales between bipolar adjectives such as lazy–energetic, fat–thin, intelligent–unintelligent, dependent–self-reliant, and so on. The investigators deliberately chose people who had not been to college, assuming these people would not be contaminated with information from previous studies that might influence their answers.

Their results:

The endomorph (soft, round) was rated fatter, older, shorter (although the silhouettes were the same height), more old-fashioned, less strong physically, more warm hearted and sympathetic, more good natured and agreeable, and more dependent on others.

The mesomorph (the muscular ideal) was rated stronger, more masculine, better looking, more adventurous, younger, taller, more mature, and more self-reliant.

The ectomorph (tall, thin, fragile) was rated younger, more ambitious, more suspicious of others, more tense and nervous, less masculine, more stubborn, more pessimistic, and quieter.

Let's examine each type.

The Tall, Muscular Ideal

"All-American male," "big man on campus," "tall, statuesque blonde": these phrases conjure up an image that represents society's ideal, perhaps even the corporate ideal. The mesomorph is the image of the person we like to look up to, the image we expect of leaders—the image of power, strength, and guidance.

Is size really an advantage in business?

[2] W. D. Wells and B. Siegel, "Stereotyped Somatypes," Psychological Reports, August 1961.

Ralph Keyes, author of *The Height of Your Life,* reports that "tall men jump higher, run faster, land more jobs, make more money, get more votes, and win more women." [3] Keyes asserts that we are obsessed with height and, consciously or not, we consistently attach values and associations to height that affect us in every phase of our lives.

Ken Cooper notes that many top executives of major corporations—sometimes perhaps as high as 80 to 90 percent—are muscular.[4] Tom Mechling, IBM's former director of corporate information, says that for visible representatives of that company—salesmen, public relations officers, corporate executives—an unwritten rule has historically given preference to tall people. You just know what image is expected for such slots.

Keyes polled some employment agencies to discover whether height affects employers offering jobs to candidates. Robert Half, president of the country's largest employment agency for accountants and financial officers, says indeed it's been his experience that tall people have an easier time being hired because "they fulfill an image, they look the part."

One executive recruiter found that, especially for high-visibility jobs—presidents, executive vice presidents, stockholders' representatives—and for more consumer-oriented companies, tallness is a prerequisite for candidates.

Perhaps you fit this category and can use the advantage of height to the fullest. The taller, more muscular body image appears more confident, outgoing, energetic, competitive, active, enterprising and optimistic, and height may be why a person is chosen for higher corporate and sales jobs. A man who fits this category is usually over six feet, strong, with a prominent bone and muscle structure. This type is decidedly athletic in appearance.

The rule that height is an advantage appears equally true for

[3] *Ralph Keyes, in* Esquire, *November 1979. Reprinted by permission of the Sterling Lord Agency.*
[4] *Ken Cooper,* Nonverbal Communication for Business Success (*New York: AMACOM, 1979*).

women. Because of the women's movement, the desire to be the petite, charming, and sexy female is giving way to efforts to be more assertive and sophisticated. For the female, lack of height may very well imply lack of clout. On the average, women are slightly shorter than men, but tall females are usually above five feet, seven inches.

All is not top jobs and high salaries for the seemingly ideal tall and muscular person. An extra-large body has disadvantages. Very tall or muscular body types can be dominating, as was illustrated by the example of Michelle. The extra bulk can create an image that is interpreted as impetuous, overly authoritative, argumentative, reckless, domineering, and even hot-tempered.

The tall person may intimidate others, who may feel, subliminally, "this person makes me feel less of a person than I would like to be." Barbara Blaes, an image consultant of the Washington firm of Barbara Blaes and Associates, has observed this response during 17 years of advising professionals on effective appearance. As she told me in a personal interview, "The person who walks into a meeting and appears to fill the room with size alone is frightening."

Of course, in some situations, such as speaking in public, the power of extra height is extremely advantageous. In general, though, the tall, apparently dominating person should tone down the image. What can be done? Like Michelle, be on guard against intimidating clients or fellow workers. A major part of the solution lies in the way you dress. Ms. Blaes advises, "Dominating, tall people should humanize and tone down their appearance. Wear medium-tone colors rather than dark, authoritative colors. Wear softer fabrics. Be careful, because fashion magazines for both men and women often picture a less authoritative image made with inappropriate soft-color suits, dresses, or jackets. Wearing a pastel plaid jacket, for example, is a mistake. Rather than just creating a less intimidating image, it detracts from the leader look. Stay with the leader image to be safe."

The best advice is to wear light suits in gray and beige with a blue shirt and a complementary tie.

The same guidelines regarding color and fabric hold true for women. Avoid authoritative suits and dresses in dark shades. Choose softer grays, beiges, light blues. Avoid large plaids or stripes as they add to size, as do higher heels. The tall female should avoid frills, busy designs, and large, obtrusive buttons. Accessories, especially jewelry, should be kept to a minimum.

Detailed suggestions are given in Charts 1 and 2.

The Tall, Thin Image

Ted Walters is the regional sales manager of a firm that manufactures rubber parts for automobiles. His job includes travel to the Midwest, and he often leads training sessions for new sales recruits. Ted's a former college basketball player and stands six feet, five inches tall. His height made him a winner on the basketball court but now sometimes presents a problem. After graduating fro college, he worked for a sporting goods chain where his flashier, brighter, and more casual image won new customers.

But now, new sales recruits feel he's looming over their heads; he's sometimes interpreted as highstrung, awkward, and not as out-going as he should be. The tall, thin look is much soght after for a basketball court or the pages of a fashion magazine, but the same thinness is not likely to help someone climb the corporate ladder. A tall, thin person is likely to convey a fast-paced, nervous, fragile, self-conscious image, and may find it dpfficult to appear assertive and authoritative.

Ted had to change his image to fit the sales world. He learned to choose suits in darker colors—dark tans, gray flannel, navy—with a slightly wider lapel to make him appear broader and slower paced. He started wearing full-pleated pants to add width to his lower torso. He changed to wider collars and slightly wider cuffs on his shirts to deemphasize the length of an already long arm. He selected shirts in colors that complemented, rather than contrasted to, his suits. Con-trasting colors helped him in the sports store since they enhanced the long, lean look of a former basketball star, but they didn't serve the same purpose in the sales group.

Chart 1. **Clothing for the tall, muscular male.**

Description: Usually over six feet. Strong, prominent bone and muscle structure. Athletic in appearance.

Advantages:	**Disadvantages:**
Appears confident, energetic, outgoing, persuasive, competitive, and enterprising.	Appears impetuous, aggressive, hot-tempered, domineering, hard, and authoritative.
To Appear Confident and Persuasive:	**To Appear Less Authoritative, Aggressive, and Dominant:**

Suits

Tan or gray flannel, two piece.	Medium-range gray or beige, two piece.

Shirts

Solid white or medium blue.	Medium or light blue.

Ties

Gray and blue combination.	Solid color to complement suit.

Shoes

Dark brown leather. Avoid heavier shoes like wing tips if you have big feet.	Tan or brown loafers.

Overcoats/Raincoats: Stay with tan and camel in pure fabrics.

Eyewear: Choose light metal or tortoiseshell frames; dark frames add to the austere look. Contact lenses are an advantage.

Briefcase: Almost any size and color is appropriate, but don't buy one that's too small.

Hints: Avoid dark, authoritative three-piece suits. Suit pants can be cuffed. Avoid pinstripes in suits and shirts. Avoid color contrasts and bright colors that call attention to height. Avoid bold patterns, plaids, and vertical stripes.

Chart 2. **Clothing for the tall, commanding female.**

Description: Generally five feet, seven inches and over. Strong, prominent features.

Advantages:	**Disadvantages:**
Appears confident, persuasive, outgoing, energetic, competitive, and optimistic.	Appears hard, aggressive, domineering, and overly authoritative.
To Appear Confident and Persuasive:	**To Appear Less Authoritative, Aggressive, and Dominant:**

Suits

Tan or gray flannel, two piece.	Soft gray, beige, light blue.

Dresses or Skirt and Blazer Combinations

Solid tan, brown, or gray. Red or navy blazer/jacket.	Light or medium blue skirt, and camel or gray flannel blazer.

Blouses

White or medium blue. Avoid frills, busy designs, and ostentatious buttons.	Lilac, pink, subtle yellows, cream.

Shoes

Wear lower heels in softer hues like brown, without fancy ornaments or ⸰ trim.	Avoid higher heels.

Blazers, Jackets, Sweaters

Red or navy.	Camel or gray flannel.

Eyewear: If you have large facial features, choose light-color frames that go with hair and eyes to deemphasize facial features. Contact lenses work well.

Accessories: A medium to large-size handbag or briefcase in dark tan or brown. Keep accessories few and simple. Avoid bows, clips, fancy trim, dangling bracelets, and large earrings.

Hints: Avoid dark, authoritative suits and dresses. Instead choose soft fabrics in gray and beige. Avoid pinstripes. Avoid color contrasts, bright colors, and large vertical stripes in blouses.

Good Combination: Medium-range gray or tan suit or dress, accented with light blue blouse. Brown shoes with low heels.

Ted learned that a thinner person should be especially careful to avoid flashy suits and watch out for pants that are too short and jacket sleeves so short that they show too much of the shirt cuff. If the neck is long collars can be a bit wider than usual to detract from the length. Vertical stripes further slenderize and should be avoided.

One of the main problems faced by the thin person is a lack of bulk. This can be alleviated by sticking with darker, authoritative colors—dark blues, tans, and grays. White or medium-blue shirts with buttondown collars rather than loose or bulky collars work well. Choose ties in combinations of red, gray or blue; slightly wider ties add width. At all costs avoid solid, thin ties. In both shirts and ties, avoid vertical stripes, which accentuate the thin look.

The thin person faces a special problem in wearing glasses. Thick, black frames prove disastrous because they emphasize an already thin facial structure. Less obvious, light-color frames that complement hair and skin coloring work best.

A recommended business outfit for either the male or the female: a suit in dark blue, tan, or camel with a complementary medium-blue or white shirt or blouse; for the man's tie, a subtle pattern or diagonal stripe in blue, gray or red.

Charts 3 and 4 give recommendations for authoritative combinations for tall, thin people.

The Small or Short Image

"Little boy," "runt," "mutt" are a few of the image-casting names directed at the small or short person. Psychologists say that these people frequently react with a need to prove themselves, and they often seem to have a chip on the shoulder.

Probably due to the stigma of shortness, several small men in history have gone out of the way to prove themselves. Napoleon readily comes to mind. It's observed also that small men choose larger wives in hopes of increasing their own stature. One recent such man was Aristotle Onassis, who chose not only more statuesque but more glamorous companions.

Chart 3. **Clothing for the tall, thin male.**

Description: Usually over six feet tall. Appears to lack muscle tone, may or may not look athletic, looks weak.

Advantages:	**Disadvantages:**
Appears gentle, youthful, serious, tactful, and precise.	Appears tense, shy, fragile, self-conscious, and awkward.

To Appear Confident, Authoritative and Persuasive:

Suits: Dark solids in navy or gray with slightly wider lapels and cuffed pants. Wear fuller pants; never wear pants that are too short.

Shirts: White or medium blue, with wider, button-down collar and slightly wider cuff.

Ties: Diagonal stripes or small designs are best. Avoid thin solids or vertical stripes; wear a slightly wider tie.

Shoes: Wear lace-ups or wing tips. Avoid long, black shoes that add length to the foot.

Overcoats/Raincoats: Light to medium tans or camel in simple style; avoid flashy look.

Eyewear: Choose medium-weight frames in tortoiseshell or brown. Avoid wire frames and dark, heavy frames.

Briefcase: A dark briefcase adds authority.

Hints: Avoid flashy jewelry and shoes. Never wear pants that are oo short. Avoid pinstripes and wide vertical stripes. Stick with solid, complementary colors rather than contrasting colors. Be dressier in general.

Good combination: Solid suit in navy or gray with a white shirt and club tie. Dark brown wing tip shoes.

Chart 4. **Clothing for the tall, thin female.**

Description: Usually over five feet eight inches. Appears to lack muscle tone; looks weak.

Advantages:	**Disadvantages:**
Appears gentle, youthful, serious, tactful, and precise.	Appears tense, shy, fragile, self-conscious, and awkward.

To Appear Confident, Authoritative, and Persuasive:

Suits and Dresses: Dark, solid colors; navy, tan, even black add authority.

Blouses: White, medium blue, cream, dark colors that complement suits. Can get by with frillier, fancier styles. Avoid wide vertical stripes; narrow, horizontal stripes add thickness. Can wear wider collars. Always wear long sleeves and avoid flashy buttons or pins on blouses.

Blazers/Jackets: Dark blue or gray flannel.

Shoes: Low heels in dark colors, closed toe. Avoid fancy buckles and other ornaments.

Overcoats/Raincoats: Camel, tan, or beige; can wear a belted waist and fuller lapels.

Eyewear: Avoid dark, heavy frames. Tortoiseshell, medium-weight frames work best.

Accessories: A medium-sized briefcase in dark tan works well.

Hints: Avoid flashy clothes; be dressier. Avoid pantsuits. Wear fuller skirts and dresses. Wear a sweater or blazer when meeting new clients. Avoid heavy, klunky accessories and jewelry.

Good Combinations: Solid suit in navy or gray with a solid white blouse. Low, dark brown shoes. Solid dress in navy or gray with a navy or dark camel blazer.

The small or short business person faces one main image problem: the need to appear more authoritative—to maximize stature, or minimize lack of height. Small people tell story after story about the difficulty of competing with larger counterparts. They want advice for appearing authoritative and powerful.

Blaes adds that another problem of the short or small person is a lack of presence. To help build an image of authority, "wear authoritative dark clothing—pinstripe suits and white shirts for men, dark suits and white blouses for women. Contrast is important; it adds dimension and depth."

Some young-looking, small corporate trainers and college professors say that, in trying to appear authoritative, they overcompensate. An extremely authoritative appearance creates the negative impression of a need to prove capability. Blaes suggests dressing in proportion to size. Don't let clothes overpower the size of the body. You may need to have your clothes tailored. She adds,

> Try to be riveting; that is, be crisp and well-defined. In the case of one professor, I recommended a dark, corduroy blazer and a button-down white or blue shirt, combined with gray slacks. This combination stated authority yet avoided the negative.

The small person might have a problem appearing mature. Wearing dark colors, avoiding bold contrast, and taking extra care in selecting well-fitted clothes alleviates the worry. Be strict and consistent, choose a conservative and dark, authoritative image, and maintain it five days a week in the office.

Some clients feel that wearing an attention-getting device such as a scarf in the suit coat pocket, or a shirt or blouse of the same color as the suit, works well. This may backfire if the device is too obvious.

The short woman faces the same image problems as the man but has an advantage: she can wear higher heels to add height. The best advice of all for the short female is to avoid bright colors and bold patterns, which call attention to her. The small female does best to stick to a well-tailored suit or a tailored dress with an authoritative jacket or blazer in navy blue. The smaller females want to do every-thing possible to appear authoritative, and solid-white, buttondown blouses or narrow pinstripes work well. Bulky frills and ties on blouses create a pinched look.

A strong, authoritative combination for the small woman is a navy or gray dress/blazer or suit over a solid-white or blue blouse with narrow pinstripes. Again, the small female can get by with higher shoes, but not so high as to make her appear unbalanced. Above all, she wants to appear neat and precise, and the charge for tailored clothes is worth the cost.

Clothing recommendations for the small male and female appear in Charts 5 and 6.

The Hefty Image

"Jolly Old St. Nicholas,""the pleasantly plump doughboy," "the circus fat lady," "chubbies are just naturally jolly": The hefty image conveys the good-natured and fun-loving spirit, even the entertainer. But beneath the jolly exterior may hide quite a different image. The hefty person is frequently cast also as unattractive, uncaring, and sloppy. The appearance of disorganization is interpreted as a sign of a lack in will power and self-control.

For the extremely overweight, dieting may be the only solution and the advice of a doctor may be necessary. With today's emphasis on fitness, the hefty person faces a real problem inside and outside the office. Extra care with personal appearance, especially dress, can make a difference. The hefty type has a problem looking neat—clothes seem to wrinkle more readily and a good fit is difficult. The solution is to spend the extra money to buy well-tailored clothes. Buy fewer suits or dresses if necessary, but invest in trusted fabrics and good fit.

The hefty has extra bulk to deal with and should not wear anything that emphasizes weight, such as tight-fitting pants, skirts, shirts or blouses, and tight belts or dresses that tie in the middle. Bright colors, bold plaids, stripes, and prints add bulk.

Chart 5. **Clothing for the short male.**

Description: Generally five feet six inches or less. Small bone and muscle structure; can be athletic.

Advantages:	**Disadvantages:**
Appears more youthful, active, and enterprising.	Appears less authoritative, assertive, and powerful; seems to lack clout.
To Appear Authoritative and Confident:	**To Appear More Mature and Sedate:**

Suits

Navy-blue or black pinstripe. Navy-blue or gray flannel solids. Three piece.	Light gray or tan solid; tweed adds depth but lessens strength. Two piece.

Shirts

Blue or red pinstripes. Solid white for highest authority. Avoid wide collars.	Light blue or other pastel. Open collar.

Hints: Stick with solid white, medium-wide, button-down collars and long sleeves; avoid wide collars that hang loose.

Ties

Subtle stripe or diagonal stripe in navy and red.	Bold stripes or solids that match the suit.

Hint: Avoid flashy colors, bold patterns, and florals.

Shoes

Black or dark brown lace-ups.	Medium tan or light tan loafers.

Hints: Avoid heavy, klunky shoes; wing tips may not work. Buy add-height shoes or thicker soles, not disco heels.

Overcoats/Raincoats: Dark tan or camel, medium collars, double-breast to add size and strength.

Eyewear: Frames should complement natural coloring; the size and shape should match the size and shape of the face. Big designer frames add too much bulk.

Briefcase: Carry a lighter briefcase in medium tan. Dark tan or black will make you appear weighted down.

Chart 5. (continued)

Hints: Match rather than contrast colors to create a flow, which increases stature and adds power. Dark colors add power and authority. Go to extremes to appear neat. Create a statement with an expensive watch. Avoid wide belts.

Strong Authoritative Combination: Navy-blue, three-piece, pinstripe suit. Solid white shirt, button-down collar, navy and red or subtly striped tie. Black leather shoes with laces, matching belt. Tan overcoat and attache.

Hefty people, male and female, should go out of the way to be neat and clean. They should select clothes in lighter, solid colors and styles that detract from bulkiness.

The hefty faces the problem of appearing unauthoritative and disorganized. For this reason, a well-coordinated wardrobe is a particular advantage. (See Charts 7 and 8.)

Tips for Building the Wardrobe of a Leader: For Men

The best guide is the clothing expected in your profession or corporation. Look around you at the people who are succeeding. What do the corporate officers wear? What does your manager wear? Is there an unwritten dress code for those who get ahead?

Take into consideration your geographic area. The Northeastern business corridor expects the blue pinstripe suit and white shirt; the West is more relaxed. Choose clothes that fit your particular locale.

Go to stores that feature quality business clothes. Buy pure fabrics in wool or cotton, or blends of wool or cotton with polyester. A blend of wool and 20 percent polyester is good for office wear or travel. Pure fabrics and fine blends cost a bit extra but wear longer and retain their shape. Buy quality rather than quantity. Two pure-fabric, three-piece suits—a gray flannel and a navy pinstripe or a dark

Chart 6. **Clothing for the short female.**

Description: Generally five feet one inch or less. Small bone and muscle structure; can be athletic.

Advantages:	Disadvantages:
Appears more youthful, active, and enterprising.	Appears less authoritative, assertive, and powerful; seems to lack clout.
To Appear Authoritative and Confident:	**To Appear More Mature and Sedate:**

Suits

Navy-blue, muted pinstripe. Navy-blue, black, camel or gray flannel solids. Three piece.	Light-gray or tan solid; tweed adds depth but lessens strength. Two piece.

Dresses

Navy-blue, black, camel, or gray flannel accompanied by complementary blazer; good combination is camel dress with blue blazer.	Light blue, tan, or other pastel. No blazer or jacket.

Hints: Small pleats (not too many) in dress or suit skirt add depth. Well-tailored suits and dresses are best; the extra charge is worth it.

Blouses

Solid white or blue pinstripe.	Light blue or other pastels.

Hints: Avoid bold patterns and wide stripes which make smallness more obvious. Avoid frills and fancy patterns.

Blazers/Sweaters: Navy-blue, gray flannel, or camel.

Shoes: Can wear higher heels, but not so high as to be unsteady; tan or black with a closed toe. Avoid shoe color that contrasts to suit or dress color.

Eyewear: Complement natural coloring; the size and shape should match the size and shape of the face; big designer frames add too much bulk.

Accessories: A smaller briefcase and purse in light, less attention-getting tans. Avoid excessive jewelry and fancy ribbons. An appropriate attention getter is an expensive watch or a simple, elegant bracelet. A nice, subtle, solid or patterned scarf in a suit or blazer pocket adds depth and character.

Hints: Stick with dark hues; match colors rather than contrast them. Add height with a full, fluffier hair style. Avoid bright lipstick and nail polish.

Chart 7. **Clothing for the hefty male.**

Description: Soft, round, overweight. Appears shorter and not athletic or strong.

Advantages:	**Disadvantages:**
Appears calm, content, sociable, and warm.	Appears sloppy, sluggish, disorganized, noncaring, and lacking in self-control.

To Appear Organized and Authoritative:	**To Appear Thinner:**

Suits

Dark gray flannel or navy pinstripe, two piece.	Light gray or tan two piece; cream color okay in warm weather.

Shirts

Solid white or medium blue or pinstripe.	Solid white.

Hint: Avoid tight shirts. Long sleeves and a medium collar without buttons works well.

Ties

Thin diagonal stripes in lighter shades of gray and blue.	Small polka dots.

Shoes

Wing tips or dark tan lace-ups. Avoid heavy shoes that add to bulky appearance.	Medium-tan loafers.

Overcoats/Raincoats: Well fitted, medium-tan or camel.

Eyewear: Choose lighter-brown, tortoiseshell, or metal frames. Avoid the beady look created by black frames.

Briefcase: Dark tan or black.

Hints: Do not wear tight-fitting clothes. Avoid wide stripes, bright colors, and bold patterns. Make an extra effort to appear neat and clean.

Good Combination: Gray flannel, two-piece suit, white shirt, and ivy-league tie. Dark, lace-up shoes.

Chart 8. **Clothing for the hefty female.**

Description: Soft, round, overweight. Appears shorter and not athletic or strong.

Advantages:	**Disadvantages:**
Appears calm, content, sociable, and warm.	Appears sloppy, sluggish, disorganized, noncaring, and lacking in self-control.

To Appear Organized and Authoritative:	**To Appear Thinner:**

Suits, Dresses

Dark blue, brown, or gray solid.	Light tan, cream, blue, gray solid.

Blouses

White, medium blue.	Cooler tones, light blue, white, creams.

Hint: Avoid frills, patterns, stripes, checks, and prints. Keep simple. Avoid puffy sleeves and short sleeves.

Blazers/Jackets

Dark blue or gray.	Light camel or gray.

Shoes

Well fitted, in dark tone, with medium heel.	Well fitted, with medium heel in light tone.

Hint: Avoid very high heels, open toes, straps, and buckles.

Overcoats/Raincoats: Light to medium tan or camel. Avoid frills, fancy buttons, and belts.

Eyewear: Light frames in brown or tortoiseshell. Avoid black and dark brown.

Briefcase: Medium tan, medium size. You might avoid carrying a purse and a briefcase, which add bulk.

Hints: Go out of the way to appear neat and clean. Avoid frills that add to bulk. Avoid bright colors, bold plaids, patterns, and stripes. Wear neutral, less attention-getting colors, like grays or tans. Wear lighter, cooler colors, even in winter. Avoid excess jewelry, which adds to bulk. Avoid tight belts.

Good Combination: Dark navy or gray, two-piece suit with a solid white blouse. Medium-high, closed-toe, well-fitted shoes.

tan—are a better choice than a dozen polyester, multicolor suits. Good fabric reflects quality and taste.

Be conservative. Avoid flashy or fad styles. High fashion is not business fashion. Buying fashionable clothes costs more in the long run because you feel obligated to change every time the styles change. A medium-size lapel on suit jackets, and pants without cuffs are always appropriate. The small extra investment for tailoring pays off.

Stick with solid-white and medium-blue shirts, or white shirts with blue pinstripes. They speak authority. Choose a fit neither too tight nor too loose. About one-half inch of shirt cuff may show below the suit coat arm. Buy one or two fancy white shirts with French cuffs and cuff links for special occasions. Avoid short sleeves except in warm climates where, to save energy, air conditioners are lowered and short sleeves are becoming more acceptable.

Buy silk or silk polyester blend ties. Wools and cottons are a good second choice. The most versatile ties have narrow, diagonal stripes in blue/gray/red combinations. Small, unimposing polka dots are acceptable business style. Club ties are passable as long as the pattern doesn't overwhelm; big patterns are tacky. Ivy-league patterns, such as a repeated diamond or circle pattern, work well with buttondown shirts, especially in conservative professions like law and banking. They usually indicate a high degree of status and education.

For authority, wear wing-tip shoes, the traditional in business. The smaller person might opt for dark-tan or black lace ups. A pair of medium-tan loafers, with or without tassels, complete basic shoe needs. Socks should be solid black, extending above the calf. Wear belts of simple, dark leather without fancy buckles, and avoid thin belts. Choose a medium-tan topcoat in camel or wool.

Tips for Building the Wardrobe of a Leader: For Women

Nancy Thompson, the image consultant mentioned in Chapter 2, suggested many of the following ideas for professional women.

1. Think carefully about your career goals.

2. Go to your closet and lay out all your clothes on your bed. Find one good, plain color blazer and one simple, skirted suit, and use them as a base. Most professional women don't wear pants on the job.

3. How many skirts do you have that will go with the blazer? Will the blazer coordinate with any of the dresses you own to create a professional look?

4. Buy a dress that is versatile. If it has its own belt, take it off, and add a belt of the same color as the shoes you'll wear. Belts should be no wider than one inch.

5. Do you have other blazers that will coordinate with other skirts or dresses? If not, add other blazers in plain, dark tones. They need not necessarily be navy or gray. Start a list: add a blazer or another suit with a blazer jacket that will interchange with the jacket or the suit you already own.

6. Remember that a jacket adds power. Create the semblance of a suit by starting with a plain blouse in a neutral color, such as black, or a long-sleeved blouse with a bow at the neck, in a color that complements your skin; add a vest of the same color, unbuttoned so that it will not emphasize the bust line. This creates a professional, authoritative look.

7. Add skirts to go with both jackets.

8. Buy blouses that button down the front, with simple collars and ties, in colors that go with many things you own. Blouses that can be worn in more than one style are preferable. In the summer, a 100 percent cotton, high-quality T-shirt, worn with a blazer, works well; it can substitute for 100 percent silk. The T-shirt must look expensive and is enhanced by discreet, fine-looking jewelry.

9. Match bags to shoes in navy, black, and dark brown, and stay with them, summer and winter. Buy good quality. A shoulder bag looks professional and frees the arms to move, and to carry a briefcase. Keep the pocketbook organized. Men often think of women as disorganized because their pocketbook or briefcase appears disorganized. Men have up to thirteen pockets in a three-piece suit; women don't have the same space and have to carry everything in one bag.

10. Jewelry should be limited to small pieces in gold or silver; stones should look like gems.

11. Wear stockings in a neutral tone that matches the skin; avoid the suntan look.

12. When thinking about how much to spend, think of quality. Divide every purchase by the number of years you can wear it. A $200 suit that you can wear for five years is a better investment than a suit costing $100 that you can wear only two years. Make sure that you can mix and match a new purchase three to four ways with what you already have. If you can't, take it back.

13. Keep in mind that men can wear the same suit for two consecutive days; if a woman does that, people think she didn't go home last night.

14. When deciding which colors are right for you, consider your complexion. They should complement the tonality of your skin. Good professional colors are black, navy, maroon, medium gray, dark gray, and bottle green.

5

Color:
A Guide to Human
Response

How does color affect the impression you make? Color preferences offer clues to personality and guide human response.

Most interesting and revealing research and theory come from color expert Faber Birren. In his book *Color and Human Response*, he looks at personal color preferences and describes how color relates to personality. The colors people select and wear consistently are a large part of their image. Look around your office. What colors do people wear? Who wears warm colors and who wears cool colors? Birren found that

> There is a major division between extroverts, who like warm colors, and introverts, who like cool colors. As to general response to color, it is wholly normal for human beings to like any and all colors. Rejection, skepticism, or outright denial of emotional content in color probably indicates a disturbed, frustrated or unhappy mortal. Undue exuberance over color, however, may be a sign of mental confusion, a flighty soul, the person who flits from one fancy or diversion to another and has poor direction and self-poise.*

* *Faber Birren,* Color and Human Response *(New York: Van Nostrand Reinhold, 1978).*

The following commentaries, adapted from Birren's book, show how color and human response are connected.

Red. There are different red types. The first comes honestly to the color, with outwardly directed interests. He or she is impulsive, possibly athletic, sexy, quick to speak the mind—whether right or wrong. The complementary red type is the meek and timid person who may choose the color because it signifies the brave qualities that are lacking. Look in this person for more hidden desires, for more sublimation of wishes than usual. Where there is dislike of red, which is fairly common, look for a person who has been frustrated, defeated in some way, bitter and angry because of unfulfilled longings.

Pink. One of Birren's studies showed that many people who liked pink were dilettantes. They lived in fairly wealthy neighborhoods and were well educated, indulged, and protected. Birren found them to be "red souls who, because of their careful guardianship, hadn't the courage to choose the color in its full intensity." A preference for pink may also signify memories of youth, gentility, or affection.

Orange. Orange is the social color, cheerful, luminous, and warm rather than hot like red. Orange personalities are friendly, have a ready smile and quick wit, and are fluent if not profound in speech. They are good natured and gregarious and do not like to be left alone. In several instances, the dislike of orange has turned out to indicate a person, once flighty, who has made a determined effort to give up superficial ways for more sober application and diligence.

Yellow. On the good side, yellow is often preferred by persons of above-average intelligence. It is, of course, associated with oriental philosophies. The yellow type likes innovation, originality, wisdom. This type tends to be introspective, discriminating, high minded, and serious about the world and the talented people in it.

Yellow in the Western world has symbolized cowardice, prejudice, persecution. Some may dislike the color for this reason.

Yellow-Green. From the few cases Birren encountered, he concluded that the yellow-green type is perceptive and leads a rich inner life but resents being looked upon as a recluse. There is desire to win admiration for a fine mind and demeanor but difficulty meeting others because of innate timidity and self-consciousness.

Green. Green is perhaps the most American of colors. It is symbolic of nature, balance, normality. Those who prefer green almost invariably are socially well adjusted, civilized, conventional. Green is perhaps an expression of Freud's oral character. Because the green types are constantly on the go and savor the good things of life, they are often overweight. The person who dislikes the green type may resist social involvement, and lack the balance that green itself suggests.

Blue-Green. Birren associated the type with narcissism, or self-love. Most people who prefer blue-green are sophisticated and discriminating, have excellent taste, are well dressed, charming, egocentric, sensitive, and refined. Where a rare dislike of blue-green is met, there is an ardent denunciation of conceit in others, the attitude: "I am as good as you are!" Or, "Who do you think you are!"

Blue. Blue is the color of conservatism, accomplishment, devotion, deliberation, introspection. It therefore goes with people who succeed through application, those who know how to earn money, make the right connections in life, and seldom do anything impulsive. They make able executives and golfers, and they usually dwell in neighborhoods where other lovers of blue are to be found. Blue types are cautious, steady, often admirable, and generally conscious of their virtues.

A dislike of blue signals revolt, guilt, a sense of failure, anger about the success of others, especially if they have not expended the effort of the hater of blue. Successful people are resented as having all the good breaks and the good luck.

Purple and Violet. Those whose favorite color is purple are usually sensitive and have above-average taste. Lovers of purple carefully avoid the more sordid, vulgar aspects of life and have high ideals for themselves and for everyone else.

Those who dislike purple are enemies of pretense, vanity, and conceit, and readily disparage cultural activities which to them are artifical.

Brown. Brown is a color of the earth, preferred by people who have homespun qualities. They are sturdy, reliable, shrewd, parsimonious; they look old when they are young and young when they are old. They are conservatives in the extreme.

In a distaste for brown, there may be impatience with what is seen as dull and boring.

White, Gray, and Black. Virtually no one ever singles out white as a first choice; it is bleak, emotionless, sterile. White, gray, and black all figure largely in the responses of disturbed human beings. On the other hand, white is the color of innocence, virtue, truth and cleanliness. White is the preferred color for weddings and for formal social events.

Black-and-white contrasts also signal upper-class status. The famous Ascot races and other social events use white and black as primary theme colors.

A preference for gray, however, usually represents a deliberate and cultivated choice. Gray's sobriety indicates an effort to keep on an even keel, to be reasonable, agreeable, useful in a restrained way. To dislike gray is less likely than to be indifferent to it. It may be that a dislike is weariness of an uneventful life, or a feeling of mediocrity.

As to black, usually only the mentally troubled are fascinated by it, though there are exceptions. Some few persons may take to the color for its sophistication, but in this preference they may be hiding their truer natures.

People who dislike black are legion. Black is death, the color of despair. Such persons often avoid the subjects of illness and death, do not acknowledge birthdays, and never admit their age.

Selecting Colors That are Right for You

1. Respect corporate of professional standards. If top level executives most often appear in navy and gray flannel, take the hint. It's a conservative environment and you will do well to follow the standard. Gray and navy are perhaps most readily associated with conservatism; bright or new tones are more liberal and may be de rigueur for fashion and design careers.

2. Don't be afraid of color. Respect professional and corporate standards, but let your personality shine through. The gray flannel suit or blazer comes to life with a scarf in the breast pocket, but to be safe, wear complementary colors.

3. Keep the season and climate in mind. White is generally considered bad taste in winter. Black absorbs heat on a humid, muggy day, but is comfortable in an air-conditioned office.

4. Complement skin and hair tones. Light skin and blond hair combined with white is a fade-out. Red hair and a ruddy complexion over violet and orange shocks. Cosmetic counselors in respected department stores conduct free color evaluations.

5. Select several colors that both complement your skin and hair color, and express your personality and buy clothes primarily in these colors. In addition it's difficult to own too many white shirts or blouses.

6. Consider the occasion. Delivering a speech at an after-six dinner meeting calls for dark, authoritative colors. Training a group of new employees might demand an authoritative, but less-threatening, gray flannel suit.

7. In choosing accessories, match and coordinate colors. Brief-cases, shoes, and pocketbooks should not blatantly contrast suit or dress colors.

The previous chapter gave guidelines for selecting clothes according to body shape and size. The following guidelines tell how to use color to alleviate a problem with body shape and size. It's actually impossible to separate clothing and color guidelines, and you should consider both to create the most effective style.

The Tall, Muscular Male or Female. Choose softer, lighter shades in gray, beige or light blues. Avoid color contrasts and bright colors that draw attention. Choose subtle combinations of blue and gray.

The Tall, Thin Male or Female. Medium-dark tans and blues

work well. Use subtle color contrasts to break a long, continuous look, a tan and cream combination, for example. Stick with solid colors; avoid bright colors and patterns.

The Small, or Short Male or Female. Stick with dark hues in blue or gray. Match colors rather than contrast them. Matched colors, especially dark colors, add power and authority. For example, a dark gray suit with a diagonally striped tie in medium to dark gray and navy is an authoritative color combination. For women, a medium-gray dress with a complementary, darker-gray jacket or blazer works well.

The Hefty Male or Female. Wear neutral, less attention-drawing colors, gray or tan hues. Wear lighter, cooler colors, even in winter. Avoid bright colors. Wear dark colors only on occasions that demand added authority.

6

Gestures and Movement: Every Part of the Body Speaks

Body language is the popular term for nonverbal communication. It often means only communication by different parts of the body. This is important, but more important is the use of gestures and movement to appear more sincere and confident, and to open or close communication. Gestures and movement that contradict what is spoken are a dead giveaway. An important question to ask about your movement is whether it adds to or subtracts from your total effectiveness. Gestures should strengthen what is said by underlining it and making it more lively, causing others to pay closer attention. If too many gestures are used, they are likely to appear unnatural and detract from total effectiveness.

Perhaps we've all observed a speaker who stands motionless behind a podium. Whether it's behind a podium or behind a desk, a static appearance deadens a message. Even minimal movement adds to visual interest and increases the credibility of speech. Coordinating gestures with your speech, whether before large groups or in conversations, requires that you know how to use every body part to enhance your image and bring to life what you say.

Picture yourself, for a moment, standing behind a podium or

sitting behind a desk. Now imagine the point of view of the person watching you and see how much of your body is free to create animation. I refer to this limited space as the *field of visibility*. In most cases, the vertical distance is about 20 to 30 inches, beginning about midchest and extending to the top of the head. This is not much space in which to create visual interest; it places a great demand on the speaker's eyes, facial expressions, and arm and hand movements to draw the audience.

The Head: Eye Contact and Facial Expression

"Keep your chin up" and "hold your head high" are two phrases that imply the importance of the head in nonverbal communication. A bowed or lowered head signals a submissive, servile attitude. The erect head makes a masterly, proud image. It immediately signals an authority in control. A lowered head gives the other person the advantage.

The face is the most expressive and revealing part of the head. We either like a face or we don't like it, and the terms we tend to use to describe faces—good or bad, beautiful or ugly, kind or cruel— reflect the emotional impact of the face.

For the purposes of discussing facial expression, we divide the face into the upper face and the lower face. Figure 6-1 shows this division. The upper face, the eyes in particular, automatically respond to outside stimuli. For example, if you're suddenly frightened or surprised, or if an insect flies into your windshield, your eyelids are likely to close automatically, if only for a second. Because the upper face responds automatically, its expressiveness is hard to control.

The lower face is more easily controlled. The jaw and mouth are largely muscular structures that can be molded into a number of different shapes. With practice the desired facial expression can be attained at will.

Eyes are the most important facial communicators. Looking a person straight in the eye has always signaled honesty, while shifting

Figure 6-1. **Control of the face.**

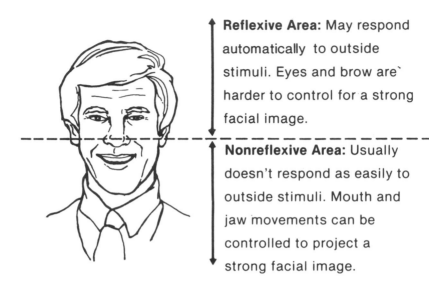

Reflexive Area: May respond automatically to outside stimuli. Eyes and brow are` harder to control for a strong facial image.

Nonreflexive Area: Usually doesn't respond as easily to outside stimuli. Mouth and jaw movements can be controlled to project a strong facial image.

eyes suggest a lack of trustworthiness. Unless people know each other intimately, they tend to glance quickly at each other, then look away; this glance is referred to as public eye contact. A look maintained too long causes the person observed to feel uncomfortable or challenged. A supervisor staring directly into the eyes of a subordinate at review time can intimidate and provoke a defensive reaction. Many freeze under such looks. If you want to make people feel inadequate, simply stare at them. The long, blank look is an outright insult.

The degree of eye contact in a private conversation is, of course, greater than in a public meeting. Eye contact in a one-on-one conversation normally occurs for 25 percent to 100 percent of the time. Contact is reduced when we carry the conversation, varying from 40 percent to 60 percent and dramatically increased to an average of 80 percent when we cease talking and listen. Avoid too little eye contact, which indicates disinterest in other people and what they have to say.

Interviews present a special case. Barbara Walters has mastered eye contact, and one of the best lessons in good eye contact is to observe her interview style. Usually seated almost directly across from the person she interviews, she maintains nearly constant eye contact. The position of her chair and her steady eye contact communicate an openness that says, in essence, "I'm interested in what you have to tell me."

Addressing groups or speaking to medium-to-large-size audiences requires a different sort of eye contact. The best advice is to form a triangle of yourself and the two far corners of the room or auditorium, as shown in Figure 6-2, and to look as you speak, not directly at the audience, but just over the tops of their heads to the far side of the triangle, creating the illusion of direct contact. Break the pattern frequently by directly addressing someone seated in one of the first two or three rows.

Eyebrows soften or harden facial appearance. The mature, wise man is portrayed with thick, bushy eyebrows. Thin, penciled eyebrows give a mature hardened image, exemplified by the pubescent girl penciling her eyebrows in an attempt to appear grown up and sophisticated. Naturally thin eyebrows on a man or a woman make a softer image lacking in presence. Concern and worry are expressed when the eyebrows move downward.

Eyelids, when wide open, are a primary signal of an alert, involved mind. The lid that hoods the eye conjures up slowness or sleepiness. The wink can be interpreted as a warm, personal gesture or as a threatening sarcastic statement. If used often, the wink becomes burlesque and signals a smooth operator.

The *forehead* can convey tension, worry, fear, and concern. A perspiring forehead indicates nervousness. A wide forehead, naturally broad or due to a receding hairline, can add strength of character. A forehead that is narrow or covered by a hairstyle gives a younger, more casual appearance.

Many people seem to have a question mark written across their forehead. This questioning expression was a real problem for one client who was totally unaware that she looked puzzled. Newly promoted to manager of her government agency, she supervised men with longer tenure than she had. Already suspect to them, she

Figure 6-2. **Public speaking to large groups.**

Eye Contact Patterns

Address the far side of a triangle, just over the eye level of your audience; you'll still appear to be direct. Break the line of vision occasionally by establishing direct eye contact with people in the first few rows of seats.

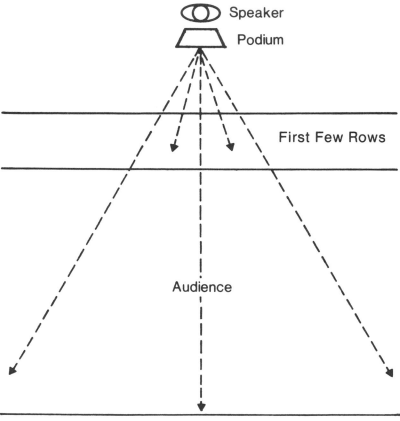

weakened her authority with her puzzled look, which silently communicated, "I'm new; I'm a bit apprehensive and uncertain, but I have the authority. Approach me with care." The solution for her image problem included standing in front of a mirror and making a concentrated effort not to frown, and several evaluations of her videotaped efforts to establish direct eye contact. Her more open, less apprehensive image improved personnel relations in her department.

The *nose* may mark the stereotype of an ethnic group. Hair pulled down over a forehead deemphasizes a large nose. But if you're dissatisfied with your nose, the most effective alternative is surgical reconstruction. Nostrils play a small part in expression. They quiver in anticipation, flare with eagerness, or widen in fear or anger.

To make the most of *mouth and lips,* learn to smile. Movie stars and politicians know the value of an open, friendly smile. They never know when a camera might catch them unsmiling and damage their public image. A smile will encourage people to see you as pleasant, warm, and open.

In making impressions on others, the mouth is a close second to the eyes in importance among facial features. We judge others in part by the shape and size of their lips. Full lips convey a softer, warmer, more sensual appearance than thin lips. Thin lips suggest firmness and strength, sometimes coldness and lack of emotion.

Lips closed firmly give an impression of strength. Lip biting signals worry, anticipation, and lack of confidence. Children thrust out their lower lips in angry defiance. Adults pout with petulance or sneer with superiority.

A most important function of the mouth is its ability to smile. Learning to project a light, natural smile is most important in image projection. A nice light smile immediately signals an open, friendly nature. The absence of a smile conveys just the opposite, a closed, unfriendly person. To verify the point, try this. The next time you're in a public place, a bar or a restaurant, speak to waiters first without smiling; later address them with a smile. Notice the difference in their service.

To find the smile that's best for you, stand before a mirror, relax the mouth and lips, and practice various smiles until you are comfortable with how you look and feel. That's the right smile for you.

The Center of the Body

Much of the power of the physical image derives from the chest area. In a standing person, the center of the body remains relatively motionless. When this area is closed off by arms folded across the chest, an unwillingness to communicate is signaled. An uncovered chest area signals openness and readiness to communicate. See Figure 6-3.

The shoulders and head combined are the best indicators of

Figure 6-3. **The center of the body.**

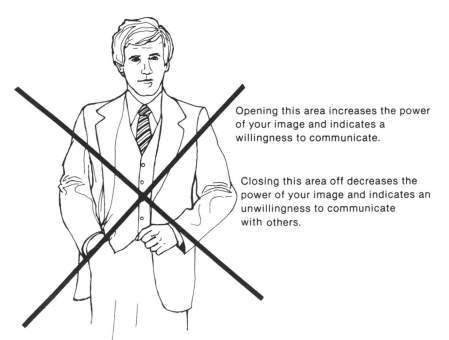

Opening this area increases the power of your image and indicates a willingness to communicate.

Closing this area off decreases the power of your image and indicates an unwillingness to communicate with others.

posture. How we carry ourselves says a lot about how we feel about ourselves. Whether we are seated or standing up, stooped shoulders convey a less authoritative image of self-dislike. Shoulders held erect mark an authoritative and proud image.

Retracted shoulders may make you appear insensitive, angry, impulsive, or domineering. Shoulders held back in an erect posture cause you to appear forceful, confident, firm and authoritative. Squared shoulders generally suggest strength and stability.

Leaning is another posture created primarily from the shoulders. Leaning forward toward another person indicates willingness to communicate. When we lean backward, we gain the power of apparent height because we appear to be looking down at others, even if they're standing and we are seated. If we lean forward, we pass the advantage to the other person. Leaning backward signals passivity, lack of control. Leaning forward sends the opposite message.

Arms and Hands

Arms signal a defensive or an open attitude. Arms held close to the body close it off and project a tense, closed image. Holding the arms away from the body instantly frees them to move and opens the vital center of the body. We either accept or reject people with arm gestures. Open arms have always welcomed or greeted others. Arm movements from the shoulder are preferable to those from the elbow because they indicate a freer, more active posture. Gestures from the elbow appear cramped and tight. Sitting with hands relaxed in the lap means preparedness to listen, while arms folded over the chest say we feel afraid or defensive.*

Hand gestures allow freedom of movement and expression. Moving the hands upward, palms toward the audience, and pulling them in toward you adds strength, while gestures that move down-

* Adapted from Ken Cooper, Nonverbal Communication for Business Success (New York: AMACOM, 1979).

ward and away from you detract. To develop an appropriate gesture pattern, stand with palms open away from you. Raise hands to the height of the shoulders. Gradually bring the hands down, palms open and up, while repeating, "I want to communicate with you." As you begin the word "I," frame your torso. As you reach the word "you," your arms and hands should be extended toward your audience. Whether you are standing behind a podium or seated across from someone at a conference table, such a hand gesture can frame your image, add height and strength to your stature, and draw your listeners toward you.

Hands consist of four parts, each of which has the potential to create meaning and complement your image: the back of the hand, the palm, the sides of the hand, and the fingers.

The open *palm* of the hand is the universal signal of peace and acceptance. Rock stars and world leaders greet their audiences by extending their arms up and out toward the people, with palms open. It's a common practice in many cultures for people to greet each other by grasping the shoulders or back with the palms of the hands. In this country, when we shake hands, we extend the palm and grip the palm of the person we're greeting. A limp wrist or a dead-fish handshake is an insult. Grip the hand firmly, sincerely.

As a general rule, avoid using gestures that show the *back* of the hand. The back of the hand elicits an image of striking; it expresses anger and disagreement.

Downward strokes of the side of the hand can be used effectively to separate or clarify points in a spoken message. Exercise caution, though, as too many chops tend to decrease clarity and credibility. Punctuation with the *clenched fist* carries the same caution. Avoid repeated clenched fist movements, as they don't add force, and they may actually diminish force, if you seem to be using them by habit.

Fingers can convey several messages in body language. Primarily, fingers signal a scold or a reprimand, especially if the forefinger juts out. If you want to use your fingers for emphasis, do not point toward your audience; direct the gesture toward the palm of the other hand, held high enough for your listeners to see. This alleviates the subtle scold. (See Figure 6-4.) Avoid using the index finger to point out or emphasize; it's more effective to group the fingers together for added strength. In general, if you do not keep the fingers together, you may appear tense and awkward.

There are thousands of hand gestures, and you must find those you are most comfortable using, a unique set of gestures that can draw attention to you and help you underline what you say. Just remember that when you're seated at a large table, or standing behind a podium, your listeners will be drawn to you if some movement adds interest to what you have to say.

To feel comfortable with arm and hand gestures, stand in front of a full-length mirror. Relax; rotate your shoulders and arms. Stretch your arms and hands over your head. Now drop them to your side and feel a new ease of movement. Move your arms and hands around your upper torso and head until you feel free to move. This usually feels very awkward at first, but becomes more natural each time you practice. Many beginners like to write gestures—set off in parentheses, or in red pencil—into their speeches and practice synchronizing speech with movement, taking one paragraph at a time. It's good to overdo gestures in the beginning and then tone them down as you become more comfortable with them.

Relax on Your Feet: Finding a Comfortable Stance

Legs and feet can indicate a firmly planted person or a rocking, self-conscious nature lacking in confidence. Stance should be erect but not tense or unnatural. Men typically stand with their feet apart; women ordinarily keep their feet closer together.

To discover your stance, simply stand up and shift your weight on your feet until you feel at ease with the distribution of your body weight. Each body seems to have a center of gravity all its own. To find this center, place your right hand on the small of your back and distribute your weight on your feet. You will probably have to shift

Figure 6-4. **Pointing into the opposite hand for emphasis, rather than at the audience.**

several times until you feel comfortable. A comfortable stance re-lieves pressures exerted by the body, permits easy movement, and allows you to stand on your feet for quite some time without fatigue.

Leg movements of a person seated are distracting and indicate tension. Foot scuffing shows insecurity and nervousness. Since many people are not aware that they scuff their feet, you should make a conscious effort to notice whether you do, and, if you do, to stop. Finding a comfortable sitting position helps alleviate the problem. Crossed legs are acceptable in both men and women, although men usually cross the ankle over the knee whereas women cross ankle over ankle. Crossed ankles are a sign of readiness, showing self-control and openness to communication.

7

Lung Power:
Vocal Images Talk
Out Loud

"That's the way it is . . . ," spoken in a calm, reassuring tone, ended the nightly news broadcast of Walter Cronkite during his entire career. His vocal image helped to create the world's most popular newscaster and the trust the public placed in him.

"Now, from Yankee Statium . . .": the twangy, nasal voice of Howard Cosell matches this phrase. His vocal image, whether coming from radio or television, is easily recognized as part of appealingly eclectic, personal sportscasting for over a decade.

Have you ever changed a radio station because you couldn't tolerate the voice of the announcer? Radio docudrama of pre-television days relied entirely on voices for character portrayal. Radio commercials still depend on vocal images, and many actors make a living using only their voices.

The voice conveys emotions and therefore influences how we feel about the person speaking. Mehrabian, a body language expert, found that people are easily able to judge a voice and determine how much the speaker likes or dislikes the person spoken to.[1]

[1] Albert Mehrabian and Martin Williams, "Nonverbal Concomitants of Perceived and Intended Persuasiveness," Journal of Personality and Social Psychology, Vol. 13, 1969.

Vocal image is also an index of social class. Upperclass British people cultivate their voices. In the United States, we make judgments about regional background based primarily on accent. The Southern drawl conjures up an image of the sweet, Southern belle and aristocratic plantation life or, less pleasantly, an image of enslavement and repression. The Yankee accent can reflect sophistication and worldliness or bring to mind the Mafia. Midwestern accents usually communicate a pleasant, unaffected style; at worst, they bring to mind a boisterous uncouth image. When we hear the Western twang, we picture the cowboy and wilderness life.

In the United States, the model vocal image leans towards the Midwestern, relatively free of stereotypical connotations. Midwestern speech is considered easier to listen to; it is faster than the Southern drawl and slower than the Yankee pace. The normal rate for American speech is 125 to 150 words per minute.

Accents, and their nation or region of origin, should be recognized. For example, the person who has difficulty reproducing the L or double L, and pronouncing it like an R or double R, is probably an Oriental. Accents, domestic or foreign, usually don't present a problem. The jet age causes people of different cultures to rub elbows, and a foreign accent often enhances more than it detracts. It can be a real advantage in cities like New York, or Washington, or other world centers where a more cosmopolitan image is expected for careers in international relations.

An effective speaking voice goes a long way toward establishing a credible professional image. Professionals find that their job demands include conversing face to face, speaking on the telephone, leading meetings, and addressing large and small groups, and that good speaking ability is a necessity.

Tools You Have to Work With

The ideal voice is smooth, free of hesitation, and clear, possesses good tone and volume, and varies in speech rate. Public speaking experts and coaches agree that speakers who control loudness, pitch, fluency, resonance, and rate of speech are thought to be more active and dynamic, more persuasive.

Although each voice is unique, each is made up of the same variables—pitch, volume, rate, and voice quality or resonance. If you're dissatisfied with your vocal image, you can change it. Compare voice improvement to learning to play a musical instrument. Just as you would spend many hours learning to play the piano, you must devote some time and effort to developing your voice.

Before you can change it, you need some basic knowledge of the tools you've got to work with, the apparatus that produces sound. Compare voice production to playing a bagpipe. The objective of the bagpipe player is to fill the bag with air so that musical notes come out easily, clear and strong; the bag relieves the pressure on breathing to produce the sound. So must your voice come out, like bagpipe notes. It is a common tendency to place all the burden of sound production on the throat and larynx, working on a choppy flow of air from the chest. The throat and vocal cords are forced to produce sound when they should be acting as resonators, producing clear sound quality. Like the bagpipe, you should fill your lungs and get the air flowing from the diaphragm, up and over the vocal cords. With this flow, you will reproduce words, sentences, and phrases as clearly as possible.

There are some good exercises for learning to breathe correctly. To do the first, lie down flat on your back. (You may wish to do this in a bedroom or other private area.) Place a medium-size book on your stomach and breathe naturally. Observe the natural rise and fall of the book. Now repeat several sentences, ad lib, tell jokes, talk to your spouse or boss. Notice how easy it is to breathe and speak.

Now stand up and imagine you're on the line in a football game. Bend over for the count, exhale, kick out all the air in your body. Now breathe and notice that you're breathing from the diaphragm-abdominal area. This is exactly where you want your breath to come from. Remain bent over, repeat several sentences, and notice the change in the quality of your voice. Now straighten up. Take your hands, wrap them around the back of your neck, gently lift your head, and then release the grip. You feel light, and the pressure of the head on the body is lessened. Stand erect, but not tense; keeping the head free, kick out or exhale all the air from your body. Exhale several times.

If you find that you still have trouble breathing from below, pretend you're a shaggy dog in 110-degree weather. Pant, stick out your tongue, and observe the contraction of the abdominal region.

It's time to coordinate sound production with breath control. Using the prior exercise, exhale all the air from your body. Hold your hand out in front of you as you *inhale* and *exhale from the diaphragm* and begin counting. As you improve the coordination of breath flow and counting, you'll be able to count up to ten or twelve. Repeat the exercise until you feel the rhythm of air flowing from the diaphragm. As coordination improves, count louder and louder, projecting your voice. Just as the bagpipe produces louder and clearer notes when the bag is filled, so you'll produce longer words and sentences more clearly and with greater ease. This exercise is also good for relaxing, whether you're to speak or not.

To improve the quality of sound production, place the index and middle fingers of either hand on your Adam's apple. Now yawn and feel the Adam's apple sink toward the back of the throat. Keep the Adam's apple lowered and speak. It's difficult at first, but notice the improved resonance of your voice. You're now ready to combine the improved breathing with the improved resonance. Relax, exhale, breathe from the diaphragm, relax the throat and speak. Repeat the entire procedure until you feel comfortable, the breath flow is even, and the quality of the voice is clear. Reread and practice the exercises until you master them. This procedure may be difficult at first, but then, so is playing a musical instrument. Practicing five to ten minutes a day teaches you to relax and to gain control of the way you breathe. You're making a fairly drastic change, and it takes time, but the effort is well worthwhile.

Characteristics of the Voice

Before we look at specific vocal image problems and solutions, it is necessary to define the characteristics possessed by all voices.

Pitch. Would you repeat that, please? If you must ask people several times what they're saying before you finally understand them, the problem is often one of pitch, of how high or low the voice is. Just as the piano has a middle C and octaves originating from it, a voice includes a base pitch and a range of variations. We ordinarily end sentences with a drop in pitch and end questions with a rise in pitch. Dropping the pitch at the end of a sentence presents a problem for the many who swallow the last couple of words. Often, the meaning of the entire sentence is lost.

Volume. The volume of your voice can be lowered and raised just as you turn the volume of a radio up or down. Volume is a sign of emotional intensity. Higher volume can reflect a more persuasive and cheerful image. Satisfaction is expressed in a medium volume, while warmth and affection are indicated by a lower volume.

On the negative side, high volume reflects tension and lack of confidence. A stockbroker who sold primarily over the telephone spoke quickly and in a high volume. To potential clients he sounded abrasive and seemed not to know his product. Investors wanted a calm, reassuring voice to place their money. As his voice volume lowered, his commissions went up.

Rate and Fluency. As vocal characteristics, rate and fluency go hand in hand. Rate is a measure of how slowly or quickly you speak. Too slow a rate of speaking indicates a floundering, unknowledgeable image. Too fast a rate indicates a slick salesperson, someone not to be trusted. Fluency is the flow, the continuity of the voice, including pauses. Excessive pauses immediately signal lack of confidence, while failure to pause signals a hurried, excitable person. A natural, flowing speech pattern lacks hesitations, reflecting an earnest, confident, and persuasive person.

Resonance. A clear, crisp, resonant voice adds force to the vocal image. Resonance is produced in the throat and voice box. Poor resonance is often called nasality, or speaking through the nose. To get an idea of the resonance of your voice, cover your ears, repeat several sentences, and listen to the voice inside your head. If it's loud and clear, you have good resonance. If it's muffled, you're speaking through your nose.

Vocal Image Problems and Suggested Solutions

The High Vocal Image

A high voice produces a tense, excited, and nervous image, indicating a lack of confidence. It's commonly regarded as feminine. In males, a higher voice reflects a nervous and artistic nature. In females, it is considered womanly and emotional.[2]

A high voice is frequently a by-product of tension in the throat. Not only is it difficult to listen to, but it places great strain on the speaker. The problem is alleviated by relaxing the throat before uttering a word. To relax before speaking—before an interview, a meeting, or a speech—let your body go limp and take several deep breaths. You need not gasp.

Another exercise that helps to relax throat and facial tension is the stifled yawn. Place your hand over your mouth and yawn silently. Repeat the yawn several times. Make grotesque faces; drop the chin, open the mouth, and move your lips from side to side. Contorting the face helps to release pressures in the jaw, mouth, and throat.

These relaxation exercises, combined with breath control, alleviate the high vocal image problem.

The Low, Deep Vocal Image

The low, deep voice is popularly viewed as more masculine, a clue to strength and self-confidence. In the male it indicates force and maturity. The low-voiced female is likely to be interpreted as manly and

[2] *Adapted from Ken Cooper,* Nonverbal Communication for Business Success *(New York: AMACOM, 1979).*

lacking in emotion. A deep vocal image does not present a grave problem unless it interferes with being understood. A deep voice may surface as a monotone, speech in one pitch and volume, which can put listeners to sleep.

Ridding yourself of a monotone requires varying the voice. Those who speak in a volume that's normal to high are perceived as more interesting, persuasive, and credible. Begin by recording your voice as you talk on the telephone or hold a casual conversation. Listen to the recording and analyze it for variation. If your voice sounds much the same regardless of what you're saying, you have a monotone.

To build variation, tape-record your voice as you read a paragraph or two from a magazine or novel. Then read two or three verses of a favorite poem; be dramatic and interpretive. With continued practice, you'll soon note variation; you sound more persuasive and interesting.

The Slow, Soft Vocal Image

In the business world, we encounter people all the time who speak so softly that we have difficulty understanding a word they say. This problem is lethal if they're leading a meeting or talking to a large group.

A slow, soft voice suggests several negative images. It imparts uncertainty and disinterest in what is being said. A slow, soft voice is a problem of volume, rate, and fluency. You know you have this problem if others frequently have to ask you to repeat what you just said. The solution begins with tape-recording the voice during a casual conversation. Listen to the recording and write out unclear words and phrases that recur. This can become your list for practicing. Record these words and phrases, breaking the words down into syllables. Open the mouth and form each syllable alone. Let the words roll out, taking care to shape each one distinctly.

Singing in the shower also helps to clear the mouth and vocal cords. The narrow walls of the shower stall, acting as a sounding board, let you hear your voice and improve the sound. The moist air aids breathing and lubricates the vocal passages.

The Fast, Loud Vocal Image

The fast, loud voice is a barometer of emotional intensity. Loud people, both male and female, are interpreted as nervous and obnoxious, or forceful and aggressive. One advantage of a loud, fast voice is that it may be viewed as dynamic and persuasive. For both the coach and the learner, it's easier to tame a fast and loud vocal image than to increase speed and volume.

The fast, loud voice is a problem of rate, fluency, and volume. Because the rate is so fast, words and entire sentences come out garbled. If you think you speak fast, tape-record yourself to find out how many words you speak per minute. Count the number of words you speak in fifteen seconds and multiply that number by four to get an approximate number per minute. The average person speaks 125 to 150 words per minute; if you speak faster, you're likely to be speaking too fast. To slow down, make a list of long sentences and long words taken from a book or magazine. Tape yourself reading them, making a genuine effort to slow down and pronounce each word distinctly. Break each word into syllables and exaggerate the pronunciation. As you continue to exaggerate, you automatically slow down. if possible, work with another person. Choose someone who can be critical, who will force you to slow down.

A fast voice is usually also a loud voice, and the same exercise helps. Another suggestion is to tape the voice as you read from a book, speaking in a whisper at first. Then gradually elevate your voice. An old trick is to match the voice to the notes of a piano, forcing yourself to stabilize the voice in the middle C octave. You automatically tune a loud voice to the moderate, ear-appealing level. Speaking loudly may also indicate a need to relax the throat; the breath control and throat exercises at the beginning of the chapter help to relieve the problem. One word of caution: loudness may result from an inability to hear your words or sentences while speaking them; in that case, you should be treated for a hearing problem.

The Hesitant, Nonfluent Vocal Image

The voice filled with pauses and "ah's" and "um's" immediately signals a lack of confidence and credibility. In the male it is likely to indicate insincerity and uncertainty, while in the female it's likely to convey weakness and uncertainty. Meaningless words, sometimes called nonfluencies, are interjections into normal speech: "you know," "ah," "um," and so on. Beginners in public speech courses exhibit this problem of nonfluency on a large scale; it usually results from tension.

If you're talking to your boss, training a group of peers, or giving a sales pitch, perhaps no single speech flaw distracts more. Credibility suffers. During lectures, I suddenly increase the number of hesitations and interjections of meaningless words in my speech. The class usually looks at me with "you don't know what you're talking about" written all over their faces. This reaction is exactly what you'll get if your conversation is filled with excess jabber.

You may not be aware that you have this problem. People commonly use excess words without knowing it. To discover if you are one of them, leave a tape recorder on while you talk on the telephone or chat casually. Replay the tape and count the number of hesitations and nonfluencies. If there are many, notice how uncertain you sound. You may want to ask someone to listen to you as you talk and point out excess words. You can also develop a habit of listening to yourself for meaningless words and for hesitations.

The best solution for this problem is to memorize verses from a favorite poem, passages from a play, or paragraphs from one of your speeches. Be sure to quote each word exactly as written; this forces you to pay attention to what you're saying and to use meaningful words instead of hesitations and meaningless words.

The Nasal Vocal Image

Nasality indicates a dull and unintelligent person. In males a nasal image connotes a lack of pride and energy. A nasal female is likely to be interpreted as dull and introverted.

Nasal image problems stem from poor resonance, or the lack of a clear, crisp sound coming from the mouth and vocal cords rather than from the nose. To test the resonance of your voice, place your hands over your ears and speak. As you talk, you'll hear a voice inside your head, much like the sound heard inside a conch shell. If the inside voice is cloudy and distorted, your voice is likely to be nasal.

The voice is most nasal when it produces words that contain difficult consonants and consonant combinations; a phrase like "double indemnity" is likely to come out very nasal. Make a list of words that contain difficult consonants, such as n, l, or v, and tape-record them, speaking with the ears covered. Concentrate on opening the mouth and forming the words with the lips, exaggerating the articulation; let words pour out of the mouth rather than the nose. Repeat the words until they sound clear inside the head. Then take your hands away and listen to the change.

Summary

The important thing to remember about vocal images is that they can be improved. A vocal problem usually incorporates several problems. Learning to breathe and to open the throat properly alleviates many of the problems; the exercises prescribed for each specific problem complete the remedy.

It is essential to *practice,* again and again. Use a tape recorder or a video recorder if possible. Form a team with someone else interested in improving, and evaluate each other. Put the techniques to work on the job; speak before groups as often as possible. For personalized evaluation and guidance, enroll in a public-speaking class or image-building seminar. Improving the vocal image is a sure guaranty of an improvement in the way others respond to you.

Part
III

GETTING DOWN
TO BUSINESS
The Corporate Focus

Your Image
Inside the Corporation

The outcome of adept handling of problems every business day adds up to good profit figures, improved standing in the business community, high ratings on Wall Street, and employee satisfaction—in other words, the survival of the corporation. The image that executives use to get results is of paramount importance both to their individual success and to the success of the organization.

Each business day is full of situations that require a convincing presentation. These responsibilities range from conversing, one-to-one, with bosses and work associates, to leading corporate meetings and speaking before shareholders and community interest groups. In many cases, the outcome is contingent on the image you project. Meetings accomplish little if your leadership style isn't convincing. Sales go down the drain. You're powerless in the face of superiors.

Med Art is a young and growing medical sales company. It faces the problem of keeping a healthy cash flow, and its life depends on every sale. The price of its products is among the highest prices in the country. Recently it sent a sales team to a hospital to make a presentation of an x-ray scanner. Signing the contract, including a service contract, would mean $1 million of income over the next year. The sales group decided on a slide demonstration, followed by questions and answers.

The group was very disorganized. They did not have the slides arranged in proper order, one person answered most of the questions, and they had left the specifications brochure at their office. Ready to purchase, the doctors felt that this disorganization and this uncertainty about how the equipment works might well indicate the type of service that Med Art gives. Their final decision: "the x-ray machine is a sizable investment. We need reliable equipment and service. We just can't take a chance."

In situations like this one, your preparation, attitude, dress, grooming, body behavior, and speaking ability determine your control of the situation, and therefore your effectiveness in getting business. Whether you're leading or participating, inside or outside the corporation, creating the appropriate image gets better results.

The outcome of countless daily situations is affected by image. Some of these situations demand an image of authority, power, and control. Others may call for less intimidating, more personable behavior. Analyzing the situation and presenting the appropriate image increases the chance that you'll get the results you want.

Corporations are places where pride and creativity, sincerity and power, competitiveness, control, aggression, and authority, or the lack of these qualities, are acted out. A corporate atmosphere contains a measure of friendliness and a feeling of family, mixed with a great deal of protection of self-interest. In its simplest outline, a corporation is a group of individuals working toward common goals: both to keep the organization running most profitably and smoothly, and to work for the benefit of each worker. To get the job done most efficiently, each person within the group must adhere to established guidelines.

Corporations consist of hierarchies, and generally the managerial level sets the climate and the pace. From the higher-level executives down through the chain of command, the corporate lifestyle sifts to all levels of the hierarchy.

No two organizations operate within exactly the same framework. Each organization has its own written and unwritten rules of expected behavior for each rank, and its own grades of status. Even in the most liberal company, which minimizes separation between the various levels, a well-defined system lets bosses and supervisors show their power.

Years of hard planning and work go into achieving top jobs, in or out of the corporation. The more seasoned executive already knows the image expected by the corporation and how to adhere to it. The younger executive on the way up is being observed every day for evidence that he is being groomed by himself and possibly by others for the higher level jobs.

Just how closely the young executive is being observed varies with the corporation and the senior executive leaders. As an illustration of an extreme, a newspaper columnist received a letter complaining about the head of a large corporation who watches his junior executives' drinking habits very closely, and promotes them accordingly. If they have more than two drinks, they're passed over for promotion—no matter how good a job they've done.

The rising executive being groomed for the top-level job is aware of the pressure from peers and superiors to fit into the ranks. Knowledge of corporate custom and respect for the deference given to rank cannot be overemphasized.

Today's Executive: On the Move and On the Make

One of the main problems faced by the rising executive or professional is the need to gain respect as an individual while working within a very structured world. There was a time when a young man or woman decided which corporation to associate with and, once the job was landed, worked through the ranks. The young executive of twenty-five years ago stayed with the same company through his or her working life; he became a company man.

Today's executive doesn't necessarily work this way. Today's executive, male or female, is more likely to be respected for mobility, for an ability to prove successful and to gain varied work experience. Early in the game, status and pay may be sacrificed for personal rewards and experience that prepare for the "job I've been waiting for."

Your image begins with accepting responsibility for your own development. You owe it to yourself to begin some strong self-evaluation. You control your own life and career. The image of the person working within the corporation must combine a concern for others with self-interest.

Despite the trend toward job changing, don't let it become a substitute for building executive ability. The balance is delicate. Subordinates and peers may be looking to you for guidance. This is a great responsibility. Superiors may look to you as potential senior executive material. The image you make as you handle everyday business tasks may lead to the top job—and to the top recommendation when you want to move to a new corporation.

You've got to have the bricks and the mortar before you can build a solid house. Now you're ready to begin construction, to look at specific, practical applications that make of image the brick foundation that supports the construction.

Your Office Reflects Your Image

For seclusion, a place to think, for reading or working at home, you probably retreat to a study or some other personal space. Your office is your personal space within the corporation. It directly reflects your level of authority, your power, your willingness to communicate, and possibly your command of respect. Corporations usually grant the more luxurious offices to executives at the top; the president rates fancier digs than the junior executive.

The arrangement of your office can control traffic flow and help or hinder approach to you. Placement of your desk, chairs, tables, plants, and sofa if there is one, can show authority or lack of it, and can draw people to you or keep them away. Figure 8-1 shows an office with good traffic flow and effective communication patterns.

As you enter, you're confronted by the authority figure, seated behind an imposing desk. A highback chair increases the feeling of authority; the two seats immediately in front of the desk are less powerful. The desk acts as a barrier separating the more authoritative from the less authoritative. Sitting in one of these chairs leaves you at the control of the person seated behind the desk.

If you are behind the desk and your objective is to retain the power position with a person of the same or lower rank, remain seated in the authority seat. Other seating patterns allow less formal, less authoritative, more open exchange. Working with people of the same or higher status might require leaving the power position and greeting them on a more equal plane.

Suppose your aim is to get the person of higher authority to meet you on a more equal basis. How do you go about it? One sales executive went so far as to drop several brochures on the floor as he entered, hoping the manager behind the desk would come to the rescue. This gave the sales person a chance to entice the manager

Figure 8-1. **The highly authoritative office.**

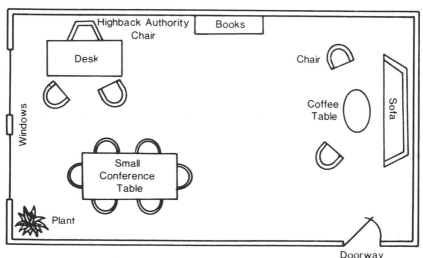

into taking a seat in front of the desk. For greater access, some sales representatives take the liberty of moving the chair from the front of the desk to the side of the desk. If you can do so without offense, ask the authority figure to review a brochure or other written piece of information that you've brought with you. An invitation to come out and look it over might lead him to take one of the two chairs in front of the desk or to sit on the sofa, assuming a less authoritative seat. Be on guard, however, that you don't offend the authority figure.

Many executives, especially in job interviews, test prospective employees to see if they will attempt to control this type of situation; they may well be on the lookout for someone who can command some authority. Others will go out of their way to meet you on a more equal plane, seating themselves on the sofa or in one of the chairs in front of the desk.

If you're seated, with a more powerful person in front of the desk, be careful not to line the chairs up directly parallel to each other. This position can create antagonism, tempting each to play the "devil's advocate." Beware of intimidation. If you're sitting on the sofa, and the other person is not, you're at a further disadvantage; the sofa swallows you up, especially if you're small. Taking one of the chairs is preferable. If there's a table in front of the sofa, and the discussion is a less formal one in which closer contact is needed, the sofa and chair combination is less intimidating.

Status levels are clearly marked in office settings. One means for gaining respect and stature is to remain standing or to lean against the door frame. If it's a quick visit—to ask an opinion, for example—remaining on your feet is a particularly appropriate authoritative approach.

The office setting can aid conflict resolution. One employee, upset by a recent separation from her husband, found her work performance hindered. Her manager, a personal friend as well as a coworker, wanted to resolve the performance problem without impairing the friendship. The manager felt she should talk the problem over in her office. When the employee first entered, the manager remained behind her desk, retaining the authority position. As she began to spell out the problem, she created a more intimate relationship by seating herself in a chair nearer her friend. After they had reached a mutual agreement about alleviating the problem, the manager moved back into the more authoritative position. Her pattern of motion from authority to less authority and return to authority allowed her to retain control while expressing personal concern.

Also recommended for handling employee relations is sitting around a small conference table in the office. Note the small conference table in the highly authoritative office in Figure 8-1. Don't overlook it as a setting conducive to resolving employee concerns, and to meeting with superiors, peers, or clients. This arrangement encourages a more open flow of ideas. If you're fortunate enough to have a small table in your office, it's a good spot for retaining the image of a leader while avoiding the barriers presented by the authoritative desk. (See Figure 8-2.)

Small tables work especially well for meeting clients. Look at Figure 8-3 and observe the ease of establishing an authoritative position simply by sitting at the end of the table. While letting you maintain authority, the small table also allows ease of conversational flow and eye contact. It's a perfect spot for examining product samples.

One hospital administrator assembles clients, employees, and mixtures of the two in this setting with good results. It creates an atmosphere that is congenial and moves business along to desired results. While he retains the image of the leader in control, participants feel free to open up and express themselves.

Control in the Conference Room

Use your image in meetings to establish status, elicit discussion, and remain in control. Some settings in the office building allow employees to meet relatively free of levels of dominion—for example, small conference rooms, the company cafeteria, or the company library. A small conference room, in particular, is a good area for resolv-

Figure 8-2. **Leaving the authority position for a more relaxed seating arrangement.**

Figure 8-3. **Working with a single client.**

ing conflicts and making decisions. Most conference rooms, however, are designed to inhibit communication and to allow a few to control it.

Figure 8-4 shows a typical conference room. Chairs arranged around an imposing, rectangular table make the perfect setup for low participation by the many, and dominance and intimidation by one or two; for lack of eye contact and little exchange of ideas. The end seats naturally command more power and authority. Fathers sit at the head of the dining table; protocol demands that heads of state sit in end positions.

The middle seats on the sides of the table allow higher participation than do other side seats. Participants seated near the middle of the table have a greater chance of getting a point across. Note that eye contact and conversation flow patterns between people seated opposite each other crisscross and are directed primarily toward the leader position. The side and end seats away from the speaker allow less participation; there is a strain to get and keep eye contact and, if the table is relatively large, a strain to be heard. Seats immediately to the right of the speaker command less attention because of a difficulty in establishing eye contact. These seats are positions of greater attentiveness and more authority. Protocol ordinarily reserves these seats for the second in the chain of command, and seats moving down the table from them for positions of decreasing authority.

Standing at either end of the table, especially behind a podium,

Figure 8-4. **Typical conference room arrangement.**

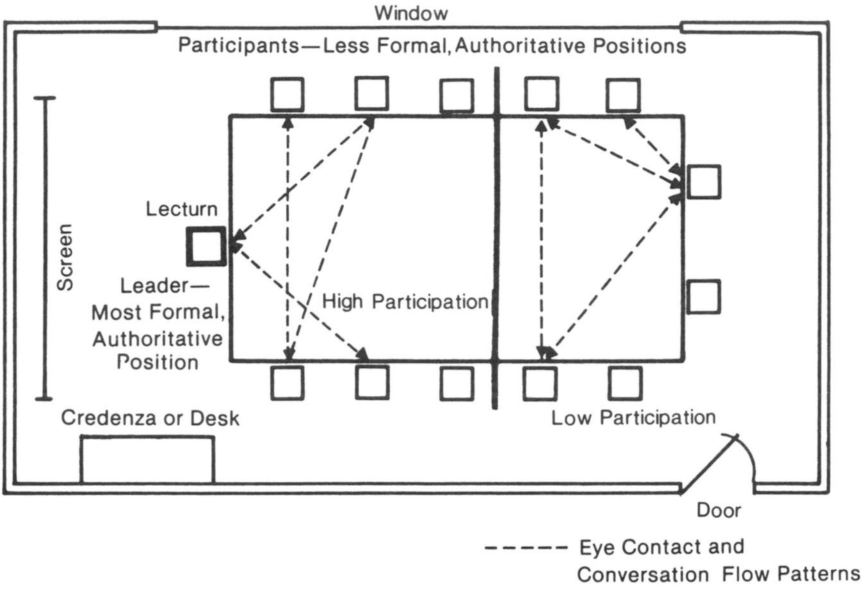

increases authority, formality, power, and control. Maintain this position unless you wish to foster greater involvement by participants. Leaving the podium and walking to the immediate right or left of it breaks authority and formality, and places greater responsibility on participants to maintain *eye* contact and to listen.

Reporting to the Board, Presenting Committee Reports

When you are making a report to superiors or leading a meeting with superiors in attendance, you're being closely observed for leadership ability. Your ability to control the meeting and to move it along to desirable results is a barometer of your image. The main problem you face in working with superiors is making a strong impression and getting your message across, while respecting their rank. You don't want to infringe on their territory, yet you can't appear as if you don't know what you're talking about, either.

These meetings usually take place in the board room. The typical arrangement seats everyone around a rectangular table. A circular or oval conference table places participants on a more equal level, as illustrated in Figure 8-5. If only a rectangular table is available, choose a seat of central authority, the middle seat on the side, or the seat at the end of the table opposite to your superior at the head, if it's available. These seats have higher visibility, indicate secondary authority, and provide the maximum opportunity for you to be recognized and heard.

To gain additional visibility and authority, stand during your presentation. Standing adds authority by placing you slightly above the group, where you draw more steady eye contact. Avoid walking around the table unless you need to walk to a visual aid. Using a podium may put you at ease, but it creates a barrier between you

Figure 8-5. **The oval conference room.**

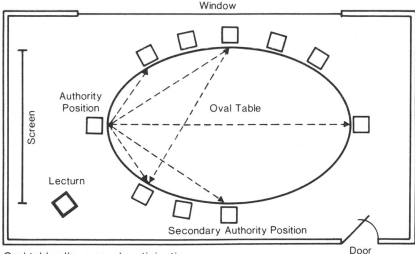

Oval table allows equal participation than a rectangular table.
Good for presentations to groups of up to 20.

– – – – – Eye contact/Conversation flow patterns

and the audience. If you simply stand at the end of the table, you will retain the sense of authority and have better rapport with the group. (See Figure 8-6.)

Wear highly authoritative clothes, as described in Chapter 4. The only problem you might encounter is appearing too much like superiors. Although most of them will respect your presence, some might think you're trying to assume their position. Prior to the meeting, find out who will be attending and their styles. If you discover that you might be offending a superior, create a less authoritative style. Wear a gray suit instead of the most highly authoritative pinstripe.

In delivering committee reports or other reports to superiors, your concern is not so much getting attention as sustaining interest and guiding the meeting toward desired results. If it ends without accomplishing much, it's going to reflect your lack of organizational and leadership ability.

In modern business, fact-finding and policy proposals are frequently delegated to committees. You may be presenting a new administrative procedure, a new accounting system, or the nature and cost of an employee training program. Sometimes reports underscore the need for change.

Thorough preparation must precede delivery of your report. Study your report beforehand and anticipate possible questions. Summarize answers in your mind, or write them out. Your goal is a concise, clearly stated, easily understood presentation.

Open the report with a brief explanation of the task, and the reasons for the report. Indicate the importance of your findings to the continued well-being of your organization.

How will the quality of the corporation's product or service be affected? How will productivity and profits be affected? If you come from a fact-finding committee, how will results affect existing policy? If you're implementing a new policy, what are the options? Which policy should be adopted? What problems are anticipated?

For variation, work out comparisons; stop for questions and clarification often. Don't get bogged down. If you run up against a

Figure 8-6. **Speaking without a podium for better rapport with the audience.**

difficult problem, rather than spending thirty minutes discussing possible answers, agree to find an answer and report back. This saves time and avoids criticism. To conclude, summarize your findings and recommend appropriate action.

Work Teams, Sales Groups, and Other Small Groups

More and more corporations, large and small, rely on work teams to get a job done. Working in a team relieves pressure on individual workers and increases commitment to the objective. Many workers are thrown into a work team with little or no idea of the way groups function or the image they should project in a group.

If all members are committed, friction should be minimal. If workers bring their individual concerns to the group and concentrate on them, the group is likely to experience difficulty. Individual needs and goals should be expressed and respected, but they must be intertwined with those of the group.

The special problem for team members is the need to compete while integrating themselves into the group. As a member, you want to express a less authoritative image, yet retain a degree of assertiveness without seeming overpowering.

You should express respect for the opinions of others. Individual goals and needs may have to be sacrificed for the good of the group; giving up your suggestion or listening to what another offers may be of advantage to the group. Team membership means taking the responsibility to come through with your part of the job. Not doing your share throws your burden onto someone else. This weakens your image to team members and perhaps to a manager observing your ability to share responsibility.

For sales group presentations, committee meetings, and team work, seating arrangements should discourage power plays and other conflicts among members. The typical arrangement around a rectangular conference table allows the stronger, more assertive members to force decisions on the soft-spoken people who may have good ideas but don't get the chance to speak up. Figure 8-7 suggests an effective configuration for a presentation to a group of clients, for a sales group presentation, for team work, and for a committee meeting. The semicircular or horseshoe arrangement focuses attention on the leader while allowing members easier access to each other. The person in authority, standing at the open end of the horseshoe, usually receives the most eye contact and the most questions. The arrows indicate patterns of eye contact and of conversation flow. The leader can lessen authority and control by moving in closer to members. Authority is increased by standing. Less formality, less authority, and more open flow is created by walking around, addressing individual participants, and varying eye contact.

Figure 8-7. **Effective arrangement for team work, sales group presentations, and presentations to clients.**

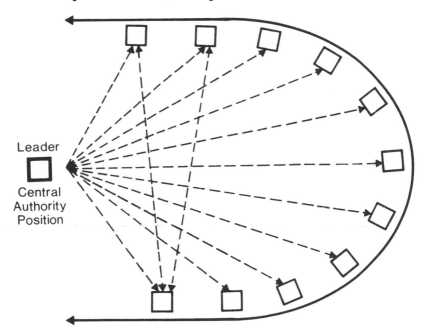

– – – – –   Patterns of Eye Contact and of Conversation Flow—Easy Interaction

This arrangement works well for participants because they at once have an unobstructed view of the leader and can maintain conversation with each other. There is minimal seating of people directly across from each other, lessening the chance of direct conflict. The usual word of caution for the person sitting directly opposite the leader: In your position, you might be taken as battling for the role of leader.

A second alternative is to meet around an oval or circular table. People are here also on a more equal plane; eye contact and conversation flow is maximized for both the leader and the participants. The leader can increase authority easily by standing, or he can lessen it by remaining seated or by moving around the table.

In these situations, the leader or participant who is speaking wants a most persuasive vocal pattern. Varied speech, pauses and gestures draw the group to the leader. (See Chapter 7 for suggestions on techniques of effective speech.) The leader may not want to talk all the time. With minimal interruption people may rise and contribute input.

Gestures should create and reinforce an atmosphere of open communication. Moving around, rather than remaining static behind the podium or standing in one spot, keeps attention. Hand movements extended toward the group indicate sincerity and willingness to converse.

The leader of the group should wear highly authoritative clothes to convey a sense of power and control. If the setting is less formal, and the emphasis less on decision making, more relaxed clothes are better. Some choose to work without a jacket, or with shirt sleeves rolled up.

Mending a Botched Sale: A Case in Point

Your client has just purchased $500,000 worth of word processing equipment from you. The client is dissatisfied, not with the product, but with the hurried, careless order, and the lack of training of both sales and service people. As the sales representative, you must keep the client happy and retain the contract.

The horseshoe seating arrangement just described is excellent for a meeting with your staff; it retains the right degree of authority and control. Handling the situation calls for an image of understanding, and control, of persuasiveness without a pointed finger. Suggested procedure: Call a meeting of everyone involved in the sale, including those who operate the equipment every day. Open with a brief re-training session that shows how the equipment works: Re-training avoids blame and name calling, and answers many questions before they can be raised by an inadequately trained, antagonistic staff. Answers also, in themselves, ease a hostile atmosphere.

Follow the brief training session with a question-and-answer period to cover questions that have not been answered already. All sides have a chance to get their feelings out in the open; yet an image of control is maintained.

Present an example of a similar organization that's satisfied with its service of the same equipment. To increase chances of improvement and gain added respect, distribute a page or two of suggestions for handling problems that might arise later, along with your telephone number. Suggest additional training for those who service the equipment all the time.

Meetings like this one call for authority and control by the sales representative. Wear highly authoritative and professional clothes.

Working with Large Groups

You may be called upon to train groups of twenty-five or more, or to lead a departmental meeting in which you want to elicit input from the group yet remain in control. One of my clients was responsible for training an average of forty new employees a month in medical terminology. He was highly educated and accustomed to instruction in a classroom; naturally, his usual procedure called for a lecture followed by a test. He ran into problems. His trainees weren't learning, and they complained that he was talking down to them. They couldn't relate to what he presented and walked out of the sessions feeling uninformed.

This situation is not quite public speaking and not quite interacting with a small group. It includes some of the problems of both. The problem is to somehow get the information out to the group, to appear in control, while remaining open to feedback and suggestions from participants. In this situation, talking down or appearing overly aggressive results in bad feelings, loss of interest, and failure to get desired results. You want to be firm and sure of yourself while concerned about member input.

Advance preparation is of utmost importance to your effectiveness. To get the most useful feedback, and the best results, send in advance of the meeting a synopsis of what you'll be covering. This gives participants a chance to come prepared to go to work.

Meetings of this type are usually conducted in a lecture format. Near the end, the leader may ask for responses from the group. Usually there's no genuine interest and response is minimal.

As an alternative format, begin your presentation with an introduction of yourself and your objectives. For example: "In my five years of working with computers, I've learned that basic misunderstanding of computer terms sometimes is the root of problems that take hours to solve. Today I want to make sure we're all speaking the same language. I welcome your input." This shows you're an authority in control, yet open to the ideas of the group.

As a leader, use a less formal approach to get feedback. After lecturing for a while, break the larger group down into smaller groups of five to seven members. Give them fifteen minutes (or longer, depending on the time you have; if you have all day, an hour is not unreasonable) to discuss the information in the lecture and to reach some conclusions on their own.

This format accomplishes several purposes: the group sees you as in control and knowledgeable, but more on their level. Because they have a chance to make an input, they are more likely to respond to you and your proposal more favorably. If they're learning new material, they learn more quickly and easily because they are part of the thinking process.

It is often useful, by the time the groups begin working together, to loosen your tie or remove your jacket, changing your highly-authoritative, formal image to a less authoritative one. Participants will see you as more willing to listen and communicate with them.

If time allows, follow the small-group activity with a short break. The break allows further, informal discussion among individuals. After reassembling, continue with the lecture or training format. Remain in shirt sleeves and open tie if you sense the group trusts you as an authority. Gauge their feelings by noting whether they express themselves freely and react to you more positively. Rather than having straight rows of chairs, arrange them into a large semicircle if the room is big enough.

Leaving the podium, seating yourself on a plane more level with other participants, and using gestures to draw them out are all important. Direct but unintimidating eye contact helps. Avoid direct pointing and prolonged eye contact. You're not scolding; you're leading.

Ask members to stand when they express an opinion. On their feet, they're more authoritative and more easily heard. As a leader, your ability to listen is of paramount importance. Pay close attention to the ideas the group expresses, and write them down on a blackboard or flip chart. Slides and other visual aids help to generate interest and strengthen your image (see Chapter 9). Whatever your means, breaking the lecture format prevents boredom and the appearance of talking down, stimulates participation, and aids comprehension.

How to Take a Reprimand

Corporate life doesn't always run smoothly. Sometimes the wrong decision is made, a budget is overrun, two hours are spent at lunch, excessive absence occurs. At these times, someone has to accept the rap, take the blame for an error.

If you're being reprimanded, it's a time to avoid increased bad feelings, to be agreeable and more submissive without appearing totally powerless. As angry feelings need to be aired, let your boss lead the conversation, and set the tone and pace.

Select a less authoritative seat if you meet in the boss's office. If you are sitting directly in front of the desk, the barrier created by the desk might be welcome on this occasion. Assume less dominating postures; a head bent slightly downward but raised frequently says, "I know I erred, but I also know I can do better." When stating your opinions, don't hesitate to hold your head more erect and maintain prolonged eye contact. Extend your hands outward in your lap to show both control and passivity. If you know of the meeting in advance, choose more submissive, less authoritative clothes. Give every intention of willingness to communicate with the superior.

How much hostility should be vented? We all at times face responsibility for failings only partially our fault. Rather than appear arrogant, aggravating already open hostility, accept the blame.

Keep the larger perspective in mind. Avoiding hostility may be well regarded later. A secretary told me of a boss who often faulted her unjustly. After six months he left his job, and she was called by his prospective employer for a reference. Her first impulse was to point out his shortcomings, as a reaction to his inconsiderateness. Instead, she recommended him, emphasizing his good qualities and only subtly indicating a couple of his weaknesses. Several years later, she was offered a position that required his high recommendation, which she got. The point to remember is that you never know when or how the person you're dealing with will figure into your life. Avoid open hostility at all costs.

Having accepted responsibility for a problem, work out a mutual agreement for resolving it. Follow up the meeting with a memo to your boss that outlines the conclusions you reached together. If your boss harbors a personal grudge, you've safeguarded yourself. If you meet your end of the bargain, and your boss still seems unhappy with you, there may be reason to believe that the bad feeling goes deeper than a response to work performance.

As a supervisor meeting with someone under you who has erred, observe the same general rules for avoiding increased hostility or bad feeling. It's your job to guide the session, point out the problem in detail, show how it's affecting the job, the department, and the entire organization, and ask for the employee's opinion. It's your responsibility to spell out the remedy for the problem, asking for input and a mutual resolution. Listen closely to the opinion of the employee. Retain a position of authority, but show that you're human.

Rewards: a Raise, a Promotion, a New Assignment

There's not a person alive who doesn't like to be complimented. Whether you're receiving good news about that long-awaited promotion or retiring with thirty years of outstanding service, you're proud and happy. So show it, while also expressing gratitude. If you're getting a raise or a promotion, more than likely you've earned it. This is an opportunity to review your future with the corporation. Show a concerned attitude by defining where you want to go within the organization. Spell out your thoughts about your career growth, and get your boss's opinion about how best to reach your new goals. Make your plan a part of your employment record or file. If you're awarded a certificate, display it in a prominent place in your office.

If the occasion is retirement or a move to another locale, and the celebration is held out of the office, after hours, a dark business suit is appropriate (unless the occasion calls for black tie). For females, the suit or dress worn to the office is fine. If you know ahead of time, you may want to dress up a bit. If the entire company or large department is present, a brief thank-you talk is expected. You're expected not to launch into a long-winded speech, but to single out people who have figured in your success, and to thank them sincerely and without fanfare.

If you're leaving for a branch office, the occasion is good for firming up associates in the office you're leaving. You may need a reference later, or cooperation in a project involving several branches. Part with the best possible record and feelings. Within two weeks after leaving, send a note of appreciation. It need not be long or detailed. Simply mention how much the working relationship has meant to you, and indicate that you want to stay in touch. If the friendship with your colleagues has been close enough, you may wish to include your home address.

Business Letters and Memos

Written materials also convey images. Jack Spangler submitted a bid that he felt sure would land a generous sales contract worth several million dollars to his company over the next five years. He felt certain that his bid was moderate enough to be accepted. Also, he had researched the client and his own competitors, and he knew he had a slight edge in product reputation. On the contract envelope, he spelled the name of the firm incorrectly and wrote an outdated address. His mistake was fatal: The contract missed the deadline.

When you write, your form is making an image. If, on meeting you for the first time, someone has told you that you're not at all like your letter, take the hint. Your written messages probably do not send the right image.

Corporations often send their executives to a business-letter-writing course or provide in-house instruction. The training needs repeating often. Correct spelling, grammar, and business format are an absolute must. The following guidelines will help you keep your written image in line. You may wish to consult a book or pamphlet, or take a course in business writing.

1. Before dictating or typing, write out what you intend to say, arranging your ideas more clearly and concisely.

2. It goes without saying: business letters must be typed.

3. Stationery should be clean. Fingerprints and coffee stains send an image of indifference and sloppiness.

4. Writing in a professional capacity means you're representing your corporation. Use paper with the corporate logo, name, and address printed on it. Many businesses personalize their stationery by printing on the paper the names of individual employees; this privilege is usually reserved for the higher ranks.

5. Promptness is important; answer business letters as quickly as time allows.

6. The greeting should bear the correct title and name of the person to whom you're writing. Be sure the title is current. Address the individual by the last name unless you're on a first-name basis. Double check the spelling.

7. The primary purpose of written messages is to increase efficiency. Use as few words as necessary to make your point. Don't, however, sacrifice clarity for brevity. Be sure to take enough space to say what you need to say as clearly as possible, but remember to be concise.

8. Avoid using technical jargon that those outside your office might not understand. For example, computer terms won't be understood easily by a drug firm.

9. Use a business tone. Be clear, concise, and direct, without being unfriendly.

10. Be sure to sign the letter, usually in the space between the complimentary closing and your name and title.

11. Make sure copies go to those who should receive them. They need not be signed.

Most companies have a standard memo form, usually printed in duplicate or triplicate. The primary purpose of the memo is to get information into the record. The person with an image of competence makes sure that memos go to the proper place.

For writing memos, follow the same general guidelines as for letter writing. Clarity, brevity, and a good business tone send an image of efficiency. You need not avoid jargon as much because those you write to are probably familiar with corporate terms. Get right to the point. Memos are for communication and recording information briefly; save longer explanations for reports.

The Secretary's Image

I often address or lead workshops in professional image for secretaries. They tell me that their image is the paper sorter, the coffee fetcher, or the typist. Their primary objective is to be perceived as serious professionals. The National Secretaries Association works hard to develop the secretarial image by upgrading the requirements, including educational standards, for moving into the rank of professional secretary. What has been accomplished already is a step in the right direction.

To be taken seriously, secretaries should act and dress professionally. Demonstrate, especially to the boss, that you have professional standards. Dress and office manner indicate the ability to accept professional responsibility, to stand in when the boss is away. If you wear the latest disco fashion, it's unlikely you'll be treated professionally or taken seriously. Especially in offices of high public visibility, wearing a suit or conservative dress separates you from the party crowd. Secretaries who work in back offices with little public contact may dress more for comfort. Dress slacks are acceptable, particularly if the climate is cold, with many months of winter ice and snow. Resolve the problem by storing a nice pair of shoes and a suit or dress in a closet at work, and change when you arrive.

How to overcome the image of a slave to a taskmaster? Be direct and serious yet friendly with your superior. Volunteer to fetch coffee under ordinary conditions, but if you're working on a rush job, don't be afraid to suggest that the boss be self-reliant. The guidelines may well vary with the boss's rank and the relationship between you. If your boss is a vice president or higher, go along with requests, particularly if there's a steady stream of appointments in and out of the office.

When you first interview for the job, ask what's expected. If you don't like what you hear, you might do well to consider another job. If you've already accepted the job, talk with fellow workers to learn the rules.

Overcoming the image of the secretary as subservient demands give and take between the executive and the secretary. Honestly drawing the line is the best way to establish a satisfactory working relationship.

Anyone who has ever worked with an incompetent secretary knows the value of a qualified and conscientious assistant. With the current short supply, many corporations recognize the importance of a good secretary, and incentives abound for an efficient one.

If you are an executive, your image around the office is made in part by the way you treat your secretary. You should take every chance to show him or her that you're grateful for a good day's work. Extend the same courtesies around the office that you'd extend elsewhere—respectful greetings and tact. A cheery good morning and frequent thank you's work wonders for boosting morale and increasing output.

Secretaries often feel that bosses expect them to play the role of the obedient spouse away from home. Treating a secretary like a spouse who can be ordered around is not only disrespectful, but reflects ignorance of corporate custom. Neither marriage partners nor secretaries like to be errand runners.

One secretary wrote to an advice column recently that she enjoys running errands for her boss; it makes her feel wanted. Her letter caused a flurry of responses. The gist of one response: how can you possibly hope to upgrade your image from a workhorse if you continue to be led by the bridle? Chores such as picking up the boss's laundry or running the boss's son to the dentist are beyond the secretary's normal call of duty. Corporations frown on the use of corporate time for personal chores: they're footing the bill.

Emergencies arise, and staying late then cannot be avoided. Advise your secretary as far in advance as possible, so that plans for the evening can be adjusted. If the work is finished at an extremely late hour, help your secretary find a way home. Calling a cab is a minimum courtesy.

How do you handle travel with a secretary of the opposite sex? A problem may arise at home if your spouse readily becomes jealous. In the office, the gossip mill inevitably starts to turn. If at all feasible, arrange for a temporary secretary in the city you travel to. If your secretary must travel with you and you end up in the same hotel, be certain that he or she shares a room with another executive or secretary of the same sex, on another floor to be doubly safe. Pointing this out will help assuage a doubting spouse.

9

In the Public Eye: At the Podium, On the Screen, and Before the Press

"As a representative of an environmental protection agency, I have to speak to some of the companies responsible for producing toxic wastes, as well as to local community groups and civic organizations, to let them know what action we're taking. The image I project determines if these groups accept our rulings. What image should I project when I address these groups?"

This is typical of the queries of many of my clients. Especially if an organization has received adverse publicity, the presentation made by a company spokesperson can determine how the organization is viewed, and dealt with.

Executives and professionals find the ability to speak well in public an invaluable asset. Corporate executives at all levels must address conventions, shareholder gatherings, national association assemblies, and meetings of local and civic groups. An oil executive may wish to defend the rising cost of gasoline, or a hospital administrator may need to explain increased hospital expenses. Building goodwill and trust, and avoiding resentment and hostility are important to the prosperity of either organization. The image of the company representative reflects the organization. It must show that the firm is honorable, that it has good intentions and good character.

William Agee, Chairman of the Board at Bendix, illustrates the importance of good public-speaking ability—in the last year he has made at least fifteen speeches, on topics ranging from social security to industrial innovation, from the Bakke decision to pension funding. He represents the top-level executive in the public eye, and the broad range of the speeches he gives shows the important role Bendix plays in creating the right corporate image. Business leaders of many large and small corporations are expressing opinions on topics of direct and indirect concern to their corporations.

Why does image figure so heavily in the effectiveness of the speaker? How you look and perform at the podium largely determines whether you and your corporation are perceived as credible. Credibility is our willingness to accept what another person says or does. Expert public speakers have long recognized the components of a believable appearance to be trustworthiness, dynamism, and expertise. Of the three, trustworthiness and dynamism rely almost entirely upon the speaker's image before the audience.

Dynamism is reflected by active and concerned involvement in the topic. Trustworthiness is determined in large part by the audience's judgment of your outward appearance. The person who appears most trustworthy and most dynamic is seen as most convincing and persuasive. Your objective as a speaker is to reduce the negative aspects of your physical appearance and enhance your stronger qualities; your image should underline what you have to say.

Speaking in public demands that you present your most authoritative and persuasive image. The clothes you wear, your general animation, the way you use your voice, and your delivery style determine whether you convince the audience.

What to Wear

Since you must appear highly authoritative and credible, you want to choose a leader's wardrobe. Males should wear a three-piece suit, solid or pinstripe, in navy blue, gray, or black. A white shirt with a coordinated tie works well; a striped tie that picks up the predominant color of the suit, combined with red, helps to garner and hold attention.

For women, a suit is the best choice. A dress in solid blue, black, or gray works well; if you contrast the dress with a jacket in red or camel, you increase your visibility from far away. Avoid prints or patterns; from a distance you may look like an abstract print.

Choose a highly authoritative blouse—white or pinstripe. Blouses that tie at the neck are strong. Limit jewelry and other accessories. Small earrings are fine; bracelets that clang on the podium are not.

For many, eyeglasses pose a problem. Ordinarily, glasses add authority and trust. But remove them during the first few minutes of the talk to establish eye contact. Do this subtly. Then replace them and continue your talk.

Posture and Movement

The most common problem with unpracticed, and sometimes seasoned, speakers is lack of animation, which indicates a tense person lacking in self-confidence. More action, or dynamism, makes a more relaxed and confident image.

For details about body movement and gestures, review Chapter 6 before speaking in public. Keep the following guidelines in mind:

Eye Contact: Select three points in the room or auditorium, perhaps just above the heads of the audience, and focus your eye contact on these points. Break the pattern frequently by looking directly at someone in one of the first few rows of seats.

Facial Expression: Practice a light, natural smile; not stiff, not clownish. Practice before a mirror until you feel comfortable. Relax facial tension before your talk by going to a secluded spot (such as a restroom) and yawning several times. Make grotesque faces. Stretch your lower jaw and mouth to loosen the muscles and get the juices flowing.

Hand Movement: At first, most people feel awkward with gestures, but you must use them. Your objective in using gestures when you speak is to invite your audience to listen to you. Hands extended before you with palms open accomplishes this purpose. Recall that palms indicate receptivity, while the back of the hand is used to strike. Keep gestures close to the body to add depth to your image and to strengthen your overall look. (See Figure 9-1.) To become comfortable with gestures, stand before a mirror and act out these lines: "I invite you to communicate with me." As you begin with the word "I," raise your arms and hands to the upper torso, palms close to the body to frame and add depth to your image. As you say the word "you," smoothly hold out your arms, palms open, to draw your audience to you. Exaggerate the gestures at first and then tone them down until you feel comfortable. The more gestures you use,

Figure 9-1. **Keeping gestures above the podium.**

the more persuasive you'll appear—up to a limit; don't overdo them or force them.

There is no appropriate gesture pattern that fits all people. Practice before a mirror or video monitor to discover the right gestures for you. Bear in mind that speaking from the podium can be static. Your field of visibility is limited, about twenty inches or so from the top of the podium to the top of your head. For this reason, gestures should range above midchest.

Avoid pointing directly at your audience to emphasize numbers or main points of your talk. Pointing has signaled scolding to most people since childhood. Also, keep the fingers closed when making gestures, to avoid the tense and awkward image of a pointed finger.

The Voice

The more expressive your voice, the better your image. Variation in your rate, pitch, and volume, combined with few, carefully placed pauses, makes your image persuasive and credible. Review Chapter 7 for specific vocal image problems and exercises for overcoming them.

Overcoming Fear

Surveys repeatedly rate public speaking as a number one fear among Americans. How is the fear of public speaking overcome? First, a few butterflies in the stomach before a speech may be healthy. A bit of fear provides the adrenalin flow needed to get you through. A major part of the fear comes from the fear of being judged by others as a failure, and the fear of being misunderstood. A positive attitude helps. Look at speech making as a chance to share knowledge and information that others want to know. Your audience came to listen to you because you have something they're interested in; otherwise, they wouldn't be there. Pretend a close friend is seated in the audience and you're conversing with him or her.

Concentrate on making your talk appeal to one person rather than think of pleasing the mass audience. Your speech is only as effective as your ability to make one person seated in the audience understand and be interested in what you have to say. If one person is with you, the chances are that everyone else in the audience is, too.

For relaxation, before the speech go to a restroom or some other private spot, and let your body muscles go limp. In particular, concentrate on relaxing the upper body muscles. Hang your hands by your side. Stretch your hands over your head. Place your hands behind your head and gently lift it to relieve the tension exerted by the weight of the head. Take several deep breaths.

The surest means for overcoming fear is practice before delivery. Many speakers think they can jot down a few ideas, walk up to the podium, and walk away wearing a blue ribbon. It's not that easy. Lack of practice results in a disorganized and unconvincing image.

Stand before a full-length mirror and run through the talk a minimum of six times. Observe your image in the mirror for facial expression, eye contact, and gestures. You've practiced enough when you can concentrate on your reflection rather than on what you're saying.

Many companies have video equipment and encourage employees to make use of it. Even without coaching, practicing before a monitor helps you see and evaluate your image.

Speech Content and Form

What you look like and how you act is the frame for what you say. The content and organization of your talk is a large measure of your degree of perceived expertness. You're judged as an expert or a novice by the way you treat your topic.

A naturally organized talk reflects a deliberate, organized and persuasive person. Speeches are ordinarily broken down into an introduction, a body, and a conclusion. The guidelines here about each area will help you. For more comprehensive information, enroll in a course in public speaking.

It's very important to build as early as possible mutual understanding between the organization you're representing and your listeners. The opening remarks should contain a statement that shows mutual respect and interest between your corporation and the audience. For example, a representative of the Environmental Protection Agency might begin like this: "You realize what our organization has done before, the legislation we've supported; our groups have worked together to resolve other conflicts. We need your support again." Or, "Mr. Wright of our organization worked steadily and hard with your people to get what we feel is a solid and mutually beneficial ruling." Statements like these, up front in the introduction, cement the audience and your organization together helping to win them over to your way of thinking.

Especially if your audience is hostile to what you're proposing, stating your purpose right away and bolstering it with facts will help erase some of the hostility. If you must mention resentments or prejudices against your organization, do so indirectly. Counter these criticisms by interpreting them in the light of your company's constructive social standing. Show that your company is presently safeguarding the public interest and plans to continue protection in the future. Introduce your appeals for support while you are showing the importance of your company's work. This moves your audience to trust you and believe you more.

As you spell out your main points, buttress them with factual information—illustrations, statistics—keeping them to the point. Avoid generalities that serve no purpose.

Language consists of words, sentences and paragraphs built upon one another to create meaning. For a more persuasive and authoritative image, arrange your thoughts logically. A well-planned pattern shows control of the subject and enhances credibility.

Style is how you use language to vocalize your image. Many speakers deliver a speech that sounds like an essay. Speeches should have a relaxed and conversational style. Using concrete, simple, and correct language gives you an image of control and confidence. New information especially should be presented clearly, in the simplest terms. Stress and repeat points for ease of understanding.

Word choice is important. Words should be geared to the level of the audience. Using large words and an extensive vocabulary may make you sound educated, but they can also make you appear foolish if they go over the listeners' heads.

Select words that say what you mean. If you use words that suggest one thing when you mean another, you're likely to be perceived as shifty and untrustworthy. Diplomacy often founders on double-speak. Wars have started because words took on unintended meanings. Your sincerity is judged by how close you come to telling the audience what you want them to know in words they understand.

The final part of a speech is the conclusion. Briefly review your main points. Make strong statements that summarize what your organization is currently doing and how it helps your audience. The environmental representative might conclude by emphasizing that the agency's objective is an improved social order.

Speech Setting

Ordinarily, little can be done to control the setting. You may know in advance only that it is a large auditorium or a room of undetermined size. Be prepared for the worst. Generally, the larger the room, the more demand placed upon your image. Appearance and animation help. Microphones improve vocal impact. If you find yourself speaking to several thousand people, at a convention for example, request that television monitors be placed at strategic points in the audience.

Time of day also affects your effectiveness. Speaking first thing in the morning or immediately after a three-martini lunch can pose a problem. If the audience is small enough and the occasion not too formal, some speakers ask the audience to rise momentarily. Of course, you can hardly expect several thousand people to stand up in orderly fashion. You might have to rely on their second cup of coffee. Better yet, rely on your image.

Consider the Audience

Fear of your audience eases with prespeech thoughts about who they are and what they're expecting from you. You should know in advance as much as possible about the audience.

The association inviting you to speak may send you a brochure or other advance that profiles those who will attend, giving you a point of reference to focus your talk. If such a description is not sent, ask for it.

Elaborate with your own profile, based partly on fact, partly on conjecture. In many cases you can guess age range, predominant sex, approximate education and income levels, and so forth. Guess what will appeal to your audience. Social scientists agree that humans are motivated by the same needs—for success, for change, for adventure and independence, for power and authority, for personal enjoyment, pride, and sexual attraction. Building appeals to these needs into your talk greatly improves your persuasiveness and authority.

Visual Aids Enhance Your Image

Sales presentations, demonstrations, lectures, and instructions in a new procedure are just a few of the situations in which a visual aid clarifies what you're saying, makes it easier for your audience to understand you, and creates a more credible, convincing image for you. You seem to know what you're talking about. But if you use the visual aid incorrectly, you may get just the opposite effect—a bungled presentation and a less convincing image.

Find out what visual aids are available, and learn how to use them. Visual aids include objects: illustrate how to fill out a job application by using the real thing. Models may include a globe of the earth or a mockup of the new corporate headquarters. Photographs, pictures, and diagrams are good visual representations of what you talk about. Charts allow you to show increases or decreases in sales with large bars, presenting a strong visual image of your point. Cutaways let us see the way an object will look and the materials that will go into it. The decoration of an office in new headquarters can be easily shown with a cutaway.

Follow these guidelines in using visual aids:

1. Do not stand between the visual and the audience—do not block their view.

2. Speak toward your audience, not toward the visual.

3. Know the visual aid well enough so that you do not have to study it while you talk.

4. As you refer to the visual, point to the specific areas you are discussing, using your finger, a pencil, or a pointer.

5. Use the aid at the point in your presentation when it will have the greatest impact. Tell the listeners what they are going to see and what it illustrates: "We're going to look at a chart that illustrates the steady growth of our company."

6. When not using the aid, put it aside, cover it up, or turn it over. Otherwise it's distracting.[1]

In preparing or selecting visuals, make certain the aid communicates what you want it to say, that it is large enough for the entire audience to see, even from the back of the room. Be sure that colors and lettering are clear enough to be seen. Finally, ask yourself whether all important parts are labeled.

Audio and audiovisual aids—that is, records, tape recordings, films, videotapes, slides, and combinations—add to your speech the dimensions of sight and sound. Nothing is more frustrating than planning to incorporate one of these items into a presentation and finding out at the last minute that something is wrong.

[1] *Roy M. Berko, Andrew D. Wolvin, and Darlyn R. Wolvin,* Communicating: A Social and Career Focus (*Boston: Houghton Mifflin, 1977*).

Test them immediately before your presentation. I allow an extra half-hour to check electric plugs, the microphone, extension cords, lighting, the order of slides or tapes, the projector, and other equipment. The more sophisticated the setup, the more time and caution needed. Advance planning may be handled by a technician, but it's still a good idea to arrive early to double-check. A run-through the night before guarantees a quality presentation.

Introducing a Speaker

When you have the responsibility to introduce a speaker, your image is on the line. You must give the most pertinent information about the speaker and the relation of the topic to the audience. You want to present the image of the speaker in the best light. Several precautions are in order:

1. Be sure of the accuracy of what you say. Get the name right. Educational background, relevant job experience, memberships, and writings should be correct.

2. Keep it short; four to six minutes is ample.

3. Let your praise be genuine. Don't build up your speaker so much that you cause embarrassment when he or she can't meet audience expectations.

4. Limit your discussion of the topic; that's the speaker's job.

5. If the speaker is already known, limit the introduction even more. In fact, no background may be necessary; introduction by name may be all that's needed.[2]

Your objective is to present the speaker as credible, yet human. When making an introductory speech, get the audience's attention and create interest in what the speaker will say. Use an anecdote or a bit of humor. Announce the speaker's topic and its relevance to the needs of the audience. Build the speaker's credibility by mentioning professional accomplishments, degrees, and writings. Also mention

[2] Wayne C. Minnick, Public Speaking (Boston: Houghton Mifflin, 1979).

job experiences and association memberships, offices held and awards won. Humanize the speaker by including hobbies, family information, or a personal philosophy of life. Incorporate a quotation from the speaker's writings, or a statement from a close friend.

Video and Television Image

"I just don't believe I look like that" is a typical response from people seeing themselves on a television or video monitor for the first time. Especially after such an initial exposure, the prospect of appearing on screen before an audience is frightening, but it need not be.

Increasingly, executives and professionals use video, if not closed-circuit television, for reporting changes in corporate policy or product line, and for bringing guest panelists and speakers, conventions, and other company activities closer to a larger audience. Video is rapidly increasing in use as a channel of corporate communication. Workers at any level never know when they will find themselves facing a camera.

By the middle of the 80's, video and television channels are expected to be the new media for conducting business, greatly alleviating the need for travel. *Teleconferencing,* or conferring through instant video messages sent between regional offices or corporations, is fast becoming a reality.

These channels, though revolutionary and rich in their potential for helping industries make money, are costly. Corporations may like the idea but are unsure about how to make them pay. It's not cheap to buy an hour's worth of satellite time or make a videotape for training. Because of the expense, some knowledge about the image before the camera is valuable. The pointers here cannot substitute for a comprehensive training session, but they can help you create your best image the next time you face a video camera.

Advance Preparation. Generally, the rules for public speaking apply. Be prepared. Write out your presentation, and if there will be an interviewer, anticipate the questions that are likely to be asked.

Begin by clearly identifying the main points. Audiences respond to only two or three ideas in any one presentation; get them out at the beginning while you have their attention.

Think about your audience. If it's inside the corporation, will it be other executives or workers from a wide range of ranks? What is likely to be their attitude toward you and what you have to say? You're competing for attention. Get and hold attention by pointing your comments directly to your audience.

If your audience is outside the corporation, you'll likely run into even more competition for attention. Anticipate a less attentive audience and present your most appealing comments first. Cite specific examples to clarify major points. If you're announcing a change in corporate policy, show how the entire corporation will be affected. Make an analogy your average listener can relate to; if you're discussing a budget change, for example, relate it to family budgeting. As in public speaking, do not think of speaking to a mass; concentrate on getting your message across to one person.

Rehearse. If you're to be interviewed, role play with someone who acts as the interviewer. Tape-record or videotape the role play. Write out tough questions and the answers you'll give. If you have adequate advance time, provide the program planner with a brief outline of your topic. Include suggestions for questions. Many producers respect advance preparation. If you're appearing on television, watch the show and analyze the format so that you'll be familiar with it.

On the Screen. Smile. You're talking to a friend—be conversational. Good facial expression is a must. Camera angles concentrate on and emphasize facial expression; lack of it deadens the picture.

Maintain eye contact with the host or other guests. Avoid letting your eyes wander. Leaning or turning toward others says you're interested. Avoid looking into the camera directly, with one exception: If you're making a point that's very important, speak directly to the camera. You're working within a smaller framework; be aware of the camera position—the one with the red light on is picking you up.

If you're making a training tape or addressing your company via video, view the camera as just another member of the audience. Speak directly to it; create a one-to-one rapport with your audience.

The scale of gestures should be less for television or video than for speaking in person. You want to scale down movements, make them less pointed or direct. A good idea for the novice is to write gestures into the script, and then practice individual segments, bringing voice and gesture together until you feel comfortable. Create a relaxed image by avoiding signs of tension—clenched fists, hands holding onto the chair or clasped in the lap. Extended hands and open palms show you're relaxed and open.

Colors on video or television are likely to show up differently than they do in a live presentation. Most studios, in or out of the corporation, use a blue backdrop, usually in a dark hue. What happens if you wear a dark suit or dress? You fade right into the background. Choose a light color; gray or camel work well. If the background is pastel, a dark suit or dress is fine. Too much dark color, especially black, blurs. Black is all right for contrast if used minimally.

White shirts are anathema for television and video. White causes glare and fade-out especially if used in large quantity. Colored shirts—in light blue, or sometimes in light green—are fine. Dark colors can work but are best avoided unless you can test them prior to the taping. Avoid patterns, checks, and pinstripes; they tend to run together on the screen.

Ties can present a problem if they have narrow, repetitive stripes of contrasting colors, say of yellow alternating with black or blue. The color combinations will appear to dance, or move before the eye, on the screen. For best results, men should choose a light-gray suit, a blue shirt, and a gray–red or gray–blue tie. Socks should always rise above the calf to prevent exposure of flesh between the sock and pants when the legs are crossed.

Men and women alike should avoid all jewelry and metal objects, such as tie clasps, that glow or shine. They are likely to reflect studio light, creating glare, or distort the image.

Women do well to wear a gray or tan dress or suit. A suit is preferred, but a dress with a contrasting jacket, especially in red, makes a good combination. If the suit is chosen, wear a light-blue or pink blouse.

Keep makeup minimal. Often someone in television stations applies a light perspiration or glare retardant just before a show. A stick or cream that erases circles under the eyes is good for men and women. If you choose to wear make-up, use a liquid or powder blush to highlight the cheeks. To get the shade or tone that's best for you, inquire at the cosmetic counter of a respected department store. Women should avoid bright-colored lipstick and nail polish.

Your Image and the Media

Your corporation, a steel manufacturer and the primary industry in your area, has just been accused of poisoning the air in your city. The headlines in the morning paper prompt an emergency meeting of executives in your corporation. You arrive at your office and suddenly a reporter has you on the phone. Or, just as you're leaving work, you come face to face with a reporter.

The best policy is polite avoidance. If you're unprepared or unsure of what you should say, you can get into real hot water. If you speak, you're representing not only yourself but your corporation. A corporation can avoid such confrontations by anticipating bad press. The public relations or public affairs department should send news releases to the papers before the damaging story appears. Or, calling an interview or news conference may be the best policy. This gives you a chance to anticipate likely questions and plan your responses in advance. Whatever your method, getting your side of the story out first may save you from being forced into the position of reacting.

If a confrontation is unavoidable and you're forced to respond, these guidelines will help you present a good image for you and your company.

1. Be direct but friendly. Don't evade questions, but don't volunteer information either. If you don't know an answer, say so.

2. Don't be hostile or argumentative. Don't disagree wholeheartedly, but don't let the reporter lead you into agreeing with a misinterpretation. Separate fact from opinion.

3. If the question is unclear, ask for clarification before going on.

4. Watch out for loaded questions. For example, if asked what your corporation has done about disposing of toxic wastes, rephrase the question before answering: "I assume you're asking what we are now doing, or what programs or procedures we're currently using." This both allows an answer more favorable to the corporation and shifts the responsibility for the rephrased question back to the reporter. It may be a good idea to meet reporters on their own level and respond, "Now, that's a loaded question," and proceed to reinterpret the question and give your answer.

Questions asked fall into several broad categories. Three of the most common types and means for handling them are:

1. Questions of policy or decision: Why was the policy made or the decision reached? An advance memo or press release alleviates many of these questions. Your response need only reiterate what has already been said.

2. Questions requesting clarification or further information. Refer directly to information from your best-informed source. Honesty is the best policy; if you're not sure of the answer, inform the reporter that your office will get back with it. Be sure to follow up by providing the information.

3. Hostile questions—designed to make you defensive. Stop. Ask the reporter to repeat the question. (This gives you time to ool off and formulate your response.) Review what your office has done previously about the matter, the policy it has established, and the stand it has taken. If possible, include a direct quotation or point out your source. Make the reporter look and feel uninformed. Explain that the present policy is in line with the corporation's overall policy. Shape your answer so that it diverts attention to the overall policy your company espouses and away from the hostile attack. This is a difficult situation. A good idea is to prepare by role playing with other executives who might be faced with the same problem. Many corporations hire outside consultants or public relations agencies to train executives who will meet the press.

Corporate Courtesies

Your image around the corporation is made of social as well as business behavior. Most of the image problems people ask me about concern how to get the job done effectively. Handling social situations is important too. Usual problems center around the roles of wives and husbands, the degree of status to expect or show and the limit for drinking at a party if you want to avoid appearing like the company lush.

On the average, we spend more time at work than at home. Yet, we seem to forget the importance of the environment we work in and pay less attention to our corporate family than to our family at home. We express ourselves to people in the way we treat them.

The Executive's Social Image

There are several preliminaries to consider in thinking about your social image in the corporation. First, keep in mind that conduct

Much of the material in this chapter is from Mila Alihan, Corporate Etiquette *(New York: David McKay Company, 1970). It was adapted by special permission of the author, who was very generous and helpful.*

codes are usually not written but that you're expected to adhere to the unwritten rules anyway. This is an important consideration for the executive on the rise who wants to meet corporate demands. Unwarranted conduct at a social event can ruin chances for a promotion. Second, your personality, taste, and interests express themselves in the way you handle social events. You want an image that reflects your personal style, yet respects corporate custom. Whether working inside the corporation or representing it in the outside world, you want your image to serve as an ambassador of good will. Third, corporations are groups of human beings, of people who experience suffering, sorrow, and joy. You would just naturally respond to these emotions in your family or among friends and you're expected to extend the same courtesy in the corporate family.

Presented here are broadly applicable expectations. Keep in mind that social expectations vary from one region of the country to another and among corporations. To get a feel for local and corporate custom, observe other executives around you, corporate philosophy, and local social behavior.

More and more, spouses, male and female, are included in corporate social events. Rules continue to change, especially for the corporate wife who would travel with her husband or enter the previously all-male bastion of a private club. To accommodate the change, airlines offer special fares for accompanying spouses.

What are the norms for the husband who must attend social events with the rising female executive who is his wife? This is fairly new territory with few precedents. For guidelines, the political husband readily comes to mind. Female senators almost nightly attend social functions, and their husbands attend with them without a problem. The wife is in the limelight and the husband does his best to complement her, with style and grace. Apply the same behavior to corporate life. If the husband attends a social event with his wife, he should conduct himself with the same decorum that he would expect in return.

The husbands and wives working in separate cities is a trend that has not seemingly experienced grave repercussions. It's not unusual for one spouse or the other to commute to another city during the work week, creating weekend marriages. Whether due to economic necessity or to a more sophisticated respect for individual career growth, couples appear to accept the trend and marriages seem to have been enriched as a result. One rising female executive pointed out in an article on weekend marriages that her relationship had grown stronger since she and her husband recognized the need to develop as individuals. When they are together now, they have more to talk about, common interests, and appreciation of the time they share together. This appears to be the prevalent attitude in such cases.

Keep in mind that, if you are being groomed for senior executive ranks, including a spouse doubles the responsibility. The way both of you handle yourselves is likely to be observed, especially if you're being considered to head a distant, regional office or a foreign post.

Sometimes spouses are not invited to attend a corporate event. A senior executive might have planned to get subordinates together for a night out. In such cases, the spouses should do their best to understand the demands of the occasion. If this situation should present a problem, one way spouses can alleviate it is to get together to play bridge or have a drink, especially if several of them know each other socially. If the occasion and time allow, the executive might salve an otherwise sore wound by having dinner before the event or a drink afterwards with the spouse alone. Many spouses are busy executives themselves and use the time wisely to catch up on extra work or attend to community or personal interests that have been neglected. Some might welcome a couple of hours to read.

Again, the same rules apply whether the executive is the husband or the wife. Generally the trend appears to be leaning more toward equal roles and a reduction in the double standard.

Choosing Associates

Because corporations exist to make a profit, they advance executives who seem most able to make money. The name of the game is competition. Many people are torn as to who to choose as friends in the corporation, who to lunch with, who to be seen with. Some employees are labeled "rotten apples"; association with a particular person may be detrimental to competitive health.

For example, a client expressed concern about having lunch with a female associate who had the reputation of being a swinger. He knew the woman only on a professional basis at the office and held her professional opinion in high esteem. Both worked in a creative advertising office and meeting occasionally over lunch would get jobs done faster. Yet, a respected family man, he was hesitant to associate with her outside the office.

He resolved the conflict—got jobs done quicker and kept his image intact—by ordering sandwiches brought in. Eventually, the entire creative department met for lunch once every two weeks in a strictly business atmosphere.

Regardless of whether we like it, we are judged by our associates. Our good intentions may be undermined by office gossip or misunderstanding. Gossip exists. The best policy: Avoid it. If senior executives are observing you, they are likely to judge your ability to stand on your own two feet, apart from the play of rumor.

If you're brought into gossip, take a strong neutral stand. Reconcile your position only to yourself and to those who are important to your career growth. Holding your own is the best remedy.

Surnames

To establish rapport, I usually prefer the less formal custom of addressing members of seminars and classes by their first names. I'll never forget one occasion when several doctors were enrolled and I addressed one of them by his first name. He retorted, "That's Dr. Jenkins, please."

Many large companies that profess a freer style demand that employees from the president on down call each other by their first names. Others demand a title and last name. What is correct?

My finding is that the rule depends on the type of business and the particular company, especially for higher level executives. In finance and other more conservative professions, established ways rule; the title and last name are preferred.

In smaller companies and in occupations with a freer philosophy—for example, fashion or advertising—first names are acceptable. These companies usually like to maintain a less formal image and a more relaxed attitude among employees. This seems to be the case especially in smaller organizations.

A good rule of thumb is to observe corporate custom or ask an insider what is expected. Usually the higher the position, the more likely the executive will be shown the respect earned. When you join a new company, wait for your boss to set the trend if you're not sure.

Beware of regional variations. The Southwest and West seem more relaxed and casual; first names are more common. In the Eastern business corridor—New York and Washington, D.C.—title and name indicate power, and the best rule is to show due respect.

A female executive may be offended by a male who addresses her by the first name, especially when they are meeting for the first time. Try to keep chivalry in bloom. The male should address the single female by "Miss" and her last name. In a poll of preferences, women unanimously favored "Miss" over "Ms.," whether written or spoken. Also, they'd rather be addressed by their surname and given the opportunity to suggest using first names. Males should wait for females to change formalities, and should respect their preference.

Behavior in the Elevator

Corporate headquarters often occupy an entire building or at least several floors. Top floors are often reserved for top ranks. This means that in the lobby you're likely to run into executives of all levels on the way to their offices. How do you conduct yourself?

Who enters the elevator first? Defer to rank. It's common courtesy and a sign of corporate respect to stand aside and acknowledge the higher rank. The same holds true for leaving the elevator; pushing the hold button shows further courtesy.

Many males still defer to females, but in this day of women's liberation, some women are insulted by acts of chivalry. If a woman strides boldly toward the door, chances are that she would prefer you not to hold it open for her.

Inside the elevator, silence rules. Conversation ceases. Heads and eyes turn and follow the lighted floor marker. A clipped hello may be in order, but that's the extent of conversation. Personal consideration and local ordinance prohibit smoking in the elevator. A polite "pardon me" as you exit is appropriate.

Clients in the Office

Offices are our homes away from home. When we receive guests in our office we should treat them with the same courtesies that we would extend at home. The image you project in your office when receiving clients, sales people, fellow executives, and executives from other corporations should reflect concern, sincerity, and courtesy.

Be prepared. How many guests are expected? Will you or your secretary greet them? If the occasion is an early morning meeting, coffee or soft drinks should be available. Seating arrangements should stress comfort and ease of interaction. You come across as disorganized if six people show up when apparently three are expected.

Remember that in business time is money. A sure guarantee for insulting your guests is to keep them waiting. Guests who leave after a five minute wait are justified. If an unavoidable delay occurs, ask your secretary to offer soft drinks or coffee and a magazine or newspaper. If you are going to a meeting and anticipate a wait, take a couple of memos or other reading matter, and take advantage of spare minutes.

Part of preparation is handling coats and other items that guests bring along. Ask the receptionist or secretary to take care of them.

Always greet visitors with a firm handshake and welcome them to your office; if you're male, it's proper to shake hands with female visitors. Make small talk with guests before getting down to business: Did you have trouble finding our building? Parking spaces were arranged for you; did you find them satisfactory?

First appearances are important; if you're a male, appear in a jacket and tie, not in shirt sleeves. If the meeting continues for some time, removing the suit jacket and working in shirt sleeves becomes permissible. The energy crisis has played havoc with air conditioning temperatures, and it's better not to work in a sauna. Let the senior executive and the circumstance set the standard. Working with a new client for the first time warrants leaving the jacket on.

Pleasing both smokers and nonsmokers, especially in a cramped office, gets to be a problem. Nonsmokers find smoke offensive; smokers prevented from smoking feel offended. Keep ashtrays ready for those who smoke. Before getting down to business, quickly polling smokers and nonsmokers, and seating them away from each other reduces possible friction.

Stop all phone calls during the meeting. It's offensive to take phone calls, and shows disrespect. Asking your secretary to say that you're in conference is adequate.

Sometimes meetings go on for a long time. A guest may just not stop talking. To handle this correctly, arrange with your secretary to interrupt after a certain time period, reminding you of another meeting or appointment. Or have her buzz you, breaking into the conversation. The most up-front way is to tell your guest that you've allotted only so much time and you have to go to your next meeting.

When guests leave, sum up the meeting. Standard procedure is to shake their hands after walking them to the door, even when they are lower-level executives. This courtesy just may be the trick that convinces the client to award your company the contract.

Telephone Image

Corporations go to great lengths to make sure the telephone is answered promptly and by a pleasant voice. One national car rental agency guarantees that calls to them are answered by the third ring and that immediate help is available.

The number of work hours, and company dollars, devoured by calls on hold is astonishing. To get an idea, assume the average employee makes $10.00 an hour and is kept waiting an average of five minutes each week. The cost per employee is $1.66 per week, $86.84 per year. Multiplied by several hundred or thousand employees, the figure puts a big dent in a corporation's budget.

Corporations also realize that the way the telephone is answered may be the client's first clue to their image. An unanswered call or an abused caller means lost business and a bruised image. Much of business and personal communication is done over the telephone. What type of image does your voice project?

How often have you placed a call and were put on hold before you had a chance to give the name of your firm? When the live voice finally returned, its tone seemed to be saying: "Why are you bothering me?" Answering the phone this way instantly creates an image of disinterest.

Use your voice to show interest. The quickest means for soothing irate callers and winning them to your side is to respond as if you care. This response erases their defensiveness and shows them that they ae on an equal footing with you.

You can enhance your telephone image by observing these basic rules:

1. Identify yourself when calling another person or a business. Use your title for added authority: "This is Mr. Snodgrass calling, Vice President of Sales for Wratchet Corporation."

2. Ask by name for the person you're calling: "May I speak with Mrs. Warner?"

3. State the purpose of your call early in the conversation: "We are holding our monthly meeting and would like you to speak."

4. Stick to the subject. A muddled call is less effective than a direct statement of what you want to know. Rambling wastes time.

5. Keep your voice firm, while showing warmth and openness.

Susan, an administrative assistant who had just applied for a transfer, received a rude and irritating call. The caller's attitude sparked her to respond defensively. Later, she discovered that her caller was the assistant to the personnel director, responsible for maintaining employee review records, including hers. Be courteous and helpful. You never know who the person is at the other end of the line, when you might meet, or how influential that person may be in your life.

Many offices of the local telephone company are willing to help you and your organization with your telephone image. They provide training geared to all levels, and asking their advice may be helpful for specific image problems.

Lunch with Your Boss or with Clients

The image you present at a luncheon should reflect consideration yet also control and authority. More than likely, you'll decide to eat in a restaurant, although you may choose a corporate dining room if you hold a rank that has access to it. Let the situation be the deciding factor; if you're entertaining a client and your company isn't equipped for fancy dining, a restaurant is the best choice.

Luncheon guests range from a boss to clients to a departing secretary you are saying good-bye to. You want an image that blends your personal manners and style with corporate custom. Your image while conducting lunch may be observed closely, especially if you're being groomed for a public contact job.

Where to eat? Consider the preference of the guests: Ask if they have a favorite. Be familiar with several good restaurants in each of various categories, so that you can readily suggest one. If they express a taste for Chinese food, for example, you should know a few good Chinese restaurants. Location and time should be considered. If your clients or boss have a full schedule, it's up to you to meet their time constraints. Don't forget to ask your secretary to call ahead (or you can call) and make a reservation.

Sometimes it's a good idea to call your guest a day in advance to confirm the appointment, especially if it's been made several weeks before. Specify again the time and place. A simple "I'm looking forward to seeing you tomorrow at 12:30 for lunch at the Four Seasons" will suffice. In one executive's experience, the client put down 1:00 on his calendar and the host put down 1:30. Luckily the client arrived a few minutes late and didn't mind waiting.

It's better to arrive several minutes before the guest is expected to make sure that all is well, especially if you've never met. Some executives establish a first-name basis with the restaurant host or hostess in order to guarantee a good seat or a more secluded table for talking business. Sometimes executives avoid serious business, such as signing a contract, over lunch. They may meet at lunch for initial contact and discussion, but they feel serious business should be completed in the office.

If you don't drink, subtly order a glass of juice or bottled water. Some people don't drink at lunch for health reasons or because of a low tolerance for alcohol. If drinking is a must, order a drink but sip it slowly, adding additional soda or water to the glass if necessary. You can avoid the customary drink before lunch by having a glass of wine with the meal. It's a good way to get off the hook; simply say, "I'll have a glass of chablis with the chicken."

Smoking can present a problem. Some restaurants now separate areas for smokers and nonsmokers. If you smoke, try to do so only before or after the meal. For the nonsmoker, smoke during a meal can ruin the taste of even the best cuisine. Limit cigar smoking especially to the end of the meal; cigars drive many people into instant wheezing. The general rule is to smoke but to respect the feelings of others by not smoking during the meal or between courses. Note whether your guests smoke. Let that be your guide; if they don't smoke, smoke less. Or ask them if smoking bothers them; many people are up front and say outright, "Yes, smoking bothers me."

Ordering the meal is usually left up to the individual diner. As the host or hostess, it's your duty to guide the luncheon. More than likely, you want to appear accommodating yet retain control; take care to consider the client; of course you pick up the tab, even if you're a woman.

For men, a conventional business suit is appropriate attire. It's not necessarily an occasion for high authority unless you're working with your boss or clients and you feel you're being observed. The pinstripe can be dispensed with unless it's appropriate to remind your boss that you know and respect signs of power. Entertaining a client, especially if you're expecting a contract or have not met before, calls for the more authoritative look.

Women should stick with conventional business attire. A dress with a jacket, or a skirt and blazer work well. A light, less authoritative look is all right for such occasions. If the luncheon is informal and attended by females only—a celebration of a leave of absence, or a bon voyage—a less formal but dressier outfit is preferable, a more festive dress, for example.

Lunches can be for social as well as business purposes—for instance, to celebrate a secretary or other employee who is leaving. Such occasions are generally more informal, and clothing and conduct can be less formal to match.

Dining in the Boss's Home

Entertaining in the home also carries different image expectations in different parts of the country and in different companies. In a city like Washington, D.C., diplomats, heads of state, government officials, and corporate executives intermingle with senators, even with the president. Socializing is an expected part of business life. It's often said that more business deals begin over drinks or dinner than in offices or board rooms.

In areas outside major metropolitan cities, the definition of social life varies. In all cases, entertaining should be guided by corporate expectations. Industrial cities of the North and Midwest often place less emphasis on socializing and friendships with other executives; business and pleasure may not be mixed. Corporation executives may be on temporary assignment and transfer after not too long a stay. In the South, on the other hand, especially in small, one-industry towns the local company may be the center of the town's social life. Stopping by another executive's home for a Saturday night drink may not be unusual.

Dining at the boss's house is a less formal occasion, when business talk should be kept to a minimum. Your boss may be observing you and your spouse firsthand to see how you handle yourself socially, deciding whether you'd make a good manager in the new divisional headquarters.

It is a good idea to know some of the interests of your boss. If the couple is socially active, you may already have good indications of their interests. As couples, you might have met at the country club or the home of another executive. If you're unaware of mutual interests, you may want to discretely hint at several topics until you trigger an enthusiastic response. Many executives make a point of keeping up with a wide range of interests, from theater to football.

Rare is the occasion when a dinner calls for a tuxedo. For the male, a dark, conservative business suit with a nice tie and dark shoes is adequate.

For the female, the simple black sheath is always in good taste. You may wish to leave the mink coat behind to avoid appearing to have more money than the hosts. The boss's wife may not own one. Avoid wearing a pantsuit, even a dressy one; miniskirts are definitely out.

If the occasion is informal, a barbecue or an outside event, dress casually. Poolside, a sports jacket and matching slacks and an open shirt are appropriate. Women often choose a longer casual dress for less formal occasions. Otherwise, a casual, but not flashy dress, or a skirt and sweater combination are fine.

Unless you're already on a first-name basis with your hosts, continue to address them as Mr. and Mrs. Soon after you arrive, they may indicate that they prefer first names, socially.

How to handle drinks? My advice is to be cautious; your behavior may be watched. Lack of sobriety indicates that you can lose control. Before leaving home, you and your spouse should decide on a limit of two drinks or even one, if your tolerance is low or if health demands it. Limit wine with the meal by sipping from the water glass. It's preferable to keep an image of control and conservatism than to establish the looser image of a person who drinks to excess.

Spouses, male and female, often mention the difficulty of making small talk with the other's boss or fellow executives. There's no substitute for being well informed. Diplomatic representatives train to keep up with current events and topics that encourage social chatter. The corporate wife or husband can adopt the same policy. Stories on the social page of the newspaper or a television feature make good conversation. It is a good idea for the husband/wife team to spend a few minutes together, while dressing or driving to the event, practicing up on current topics of interest. One rule seems to apply across the board: Avoid talking business, especially touchy problems related to the corporation itself. It's a dead giveaway of your spouse's feelings, and may be just the bit of gossip an eager rival might want to carry directly to a more powerful executive.

Discussion of business should be guided by your boss. Since the occasion is social, business is not likely to come up and, if it does, only briefly. When executives are all males, they tend to separate sometimes from the ladies and briefly discuss business. It's not your place to mention business to your boss or dig for information. You wouldn't go to your doctor's house for dinner and discuss your headache. Leave business problems in the office.

A good rule of thumb is to note and adhere strictly to the time on the invitation. If the dinner invitation reads 7:30 until 11:00 P.M., be on time. Dinner requires scheduling and a serving time may be strictly observed. If you're invited for cocktails only, there's some leeway. Arriving five minutes late is acceptable. Be prompt about leaving as well; don't overstay your welcome. Within ten days of a dinner, send a thank-you note.

Having the Boss Over for Dinner

If you know you're being groomed for a promotion or just want to be liked by your boss, a dinner invitation is a good way to break the ice. Your image should not outshine the boss's; it should represent your level in the corporation.

For dinner in your home, extend the invitation early enough for your boss to fit the date into a busy schedule—at least two weeks in advance. The invitation should clearly spell out the date, the time, your address, and your telephone number. If you live in an area of town unfamiliar to your boss, you may want to include a small map or instructions. If the occasion is to be more casual—a poolside dinner or a backyard barbecue—indicate it on the invitation. Otherwise, the boss will assume the dinner is sitdown.

This may be a good time to hire help for serving, especially if your boss had help when entertaining you. This relieves you from some of the more mundane duties and frees you to entertain. Many couples choose to serve drinks and to let the help handle only the appetizers and food. The way your boss has entertained you should guide you.

Although you're at home and usually entertain in a more casual style, this occasion requires a suit and tie. Choose a comfortable one. A darker business suit is best. Don't wear your peach polyester or lime-green leisure suit with an Hawaiian open shirt and a gold chain. A certain amount of decorum is expected. For the female, a nice dark dress works best. Avoid a casual outfit, a pantsuit, or a fancy dress.

The primary idea is not to outshine the boss. Choose your good silver and china but don't overdo the display. Follow the same guidelines for social chatter that you use at the boss's house. Stick with topics of general current interest. Avoid talking about business and controversial issues.

Corporate Parties

Corporate parties vary from the annual Christmas party to those that honor an anniversary of the corporation's foundation or the departure of an executive for a foreign post or a field office. Some are more relaxed and casual, while others have more formal rules of behavior.

Again, conservatism is the best policy. Minimize drinking, avoid business talk, and keep behavior up to corporate expectations. Rules of behavior are generally unwritten. The following discussion of the company Christmas party is offered as a guide. You may have to adapt the ideas to suit the expectations of your particular region and corporation.

Some corporations hold separate Christmas parties for employees and their children; others combine the two. Some companies pay the entire bill; others won't touch it.

Instruct your children to display their best manners, and especially to thank the appropriate executives. Impress on them that this is no ordinary party, and they should put their best foot forward.

Christmas parties are the big events of the year, especially in companies in small towns or for employees who do not socialize often. They're usually anticipated with a great deal of joy.

The trend is to invite spouses, and food and liquor usually abound. In the back of your mind be conscious that an important corporate officer might be present and observing the way you handle yourself. Both you and your spouse should minimize drinking. Keep a highball in hand but sip cautiously; add ice and water to keep up the appearance of friendly conviviality.

Some corporations, especially in small towns or family-oriented businesses, prefer a more private party, reserved for management. At such parties special care should be taken to observe the rules about drinking and behavior. Also, more formal wear might be in order, even a black tie for the man and a gown and stole for the woman.

Clothing for Evening

Some occasions call for a tuxedo, or gown and fur—more formal clothes. Often the invitation will indicate what is expected. If you're uncertain, ask.

You need not buy a tuxedo for only one or two events a year. Most towns have at least one formal-wear rental shop where you can rent a dress shirt and tux, and even formal shoes.

For women it's a different story. There's almost no way to get around owning one or two evening gowns—a full-length gown for more formal events, and a full, below-the-knee gown for receptions and cocktail parties. Local custom usually dictates what's appropriate. Also, you must use foresight. For example, if you're attending a reception with the mayor and other notables from the corporation and the local community, wear the more formal, full-length gown. The reception may be just the beginning of an evening when formal wear is expected throughout.

Choosing an appropriate gown should be discussed with someone in a reputable local department store. Formal wear is naturally expected of anyone who has reached a certain level of success. It can be worn more than once. Most women are ingenious enough to vary a gown slightly. Adding a belt or a broach, even a corsage, can create a new look. In these days of tight family budgets, many women are not ashamed of buying a second or third gown from a shop that recycles. For a fraction of the original cost, they find a dress that has been worn only once or twice and is totally new for them and the occasion.

How to Handle Business-Social Communications

Bread-and-Butter Notes: Thank You. Thank-you notes are not used as much today as they were 50 years ago. A hearty thank you at the door after a pleasant evening is considered adequate. Sometimes the guests telephone the hosts the next day and express their appreciation.

When a couple are guests at a dinner party arranged in their honor, so that they can meet associates or important corporate members, a note of appreciation expressing thanks is sure to win a favorable reaction. For an overnight or weekend stay, a thank-you note is mandatory.

There are regional variations. A thank-you note might be expected for almost any occasion in the more aristocratic South or in cities where association with diplomats or other prestigious outsiders is more common. In these cases, it's best to send a note.

Winning a Contract. If someone wins a contract, a congratulatory message is in order, especially if you hope that person will be or will continue to be your client. Business etiquette encourages sending such a message even to an executive not known to you personally but whose favor you want to cultivate.

Promotions. Any status or job change should be felicitated with congratulations and good wishes.

Corporate Anniversaries. Whether or not you're invited to attend the celebration, you need not overlook the occasion of another firm's corporate anniversary. Send a telegram or a congratulatory letter to any executives you know there, expressing best wishes for continued success.

Personnel Recognition. Corporations usually mark the 10th, 20th, and 25th anniversaries of an employee's tenure with a celebration and perhaps a gift. Even if you sign a department card and contribute to a gift, a personal note is welcomed.

Engagements, Weddings. An announcement of an engagement, a wedding, or a birth should be acknowledged with a congratulatory card, or—if the relationship is a close one—a gift.

No executive with business savvy can afford to ignore an invitation to a wedding. Unless you're out of town, try to accept all invitations to the weddings of employees reporting to you, or of other executives of your rank. Attending weddings in the family of a superior depends on local and corporate custom. You shouldn't appear out of place, yet attendance may be good public relations. The same rules apply to weddings of clients. If you work directly with the client, you might feel comfortable going. If the invitation is merely a courtesy, let the custom of your corporation determine whether or not you attend.

As a guideline: send gifts if you're invited to the reception. Use discretion otherwise: if you feel it would be helpful for personal public relations, send a gift.

Illness. When members of the corporation are ill or confined to the home or the hospital, some expression of good cheer and encouragement is in order. Cards, sent at two-week intervals, are recommended. For flowers, some consideration should be given to specifically male or female arrangements, and to hospital limitations. Many florists solve these problems for you; potted plants in particular are more easily handled in a hospital.

When the illness is terminal, observe the guidelines set by the immediate family. The rules vary, and local and family tradition should help you. In one company, the patient's entire department, including supervisors, made sure fresh flowers were sent every week. On the other hand, if the patient is too ill, or if the family expressly discourages weekly arrangements, they are inappropriate.

Corporate Disaster. Disastrous circumstances are usually handled by a note from the president of your company to the head of the afflicted corporation. If you know a person involved, such as a client, a note of concern is in order.

Death of an Executive in Another Company. Letters of condolence are generally handwritten, but the typewritten letter is acceptable for a business associate. A telegram may be sent. Such messages should ordinarily go to the person's immediate superior or to the next of "business kin." If the deceased is a customer or valued friend, condolences to the family are in good taste.

Death Within Your Own Corporation. When a member of your own management or one of your subordinates dies, pay your respects to the family. Depending on the special arrangements, you can attend either the church services or those at the funeral chapel. If you were close, going to the cemetery and visiting the family's home afterward may be expected.

If the family does not want flowers, the obituary notice usually states, "Omit flowers." If they're acceptable, send a spray or wreath. Some corporate teams or departments send flowers as a group, and if you are a member, you are expected to participate. Help with the cost and sign the card that accompanies the arrangement. When the relationship is more personal, many elect to send flowers directly to the home, especially if encouraged by religious custom.

Religious customs should be observed. Be sure to check religious preference and adhere to standard guidelines. Because circumstances are so widely varied, the best advice is to check local expectations. A call to the funeral home or to your religious advisor can provide the answer.

If the death occurs in your family, acknowledge receipt of flowers and cards, or donations of food or money. Personalized, handwritten cards are preferable but printed or engraved cards are acceptable.

Membership in the Country Club and Your Image

The importance of country club membership varies with the region of the country, the size of the city, and corporate expectations. In smaller cities in remote areas, country club memberships are necessary for status and social image, as a membership is prestigious in the community. Spending time at the club is an easy way to meet other executives and local business people or to learn about community concerns. You often learn more over a drink at the club than through a telephone call from your office. In the smaller city, the relaxation or exercise routine may well be merged with business.

It may also be easier to entertain at the club. Some small towns have few restaurants, and the club is a good substitute. The corporate lifestyle is often reflected in club life; in the way executives play bridge or form golf partnerships.

In larger cities, community concerns are often not discussed at the club. Executives often use the club to escape business and don't want to be bothered there. For them it's a place to relax and play a round of golf, take a swim, or play tennis without business pressures.

In most cases, membership in a country club enhances the image. The best advice: look around to see what is expected. Join if you'll benefit and if your company expects it. But if you're using the membership as a passport to success, you may run into problems.

Part
IV

SELF-PROMOTION
Keep Your Image
in the Limelight

Creating Visibility

If all you do is dream about success, success will remain a dream. The dedicated professional, out to get the most in a career, doesn't sit idly by and wait for success to happen. At any age, in or out of a corporation, those who turn dreams into reality accept the responsibility for self-improvement and career growth. Those in the mainstream take control and gauge career development often, to guarantee they're headed in the right direction. One way to safeguard career growth is self-promotion.

Making Networks

One aspect of self-promotion is networking—creating and maintaining a system of contacts. Networking is not a new idea; men's clubs and the buddy system have been around a long time. Business owners use networks to establish clients and mailing lists. However, networks are relatively new for some career women, and several books and networking organizations have sprung up as a result. You may want to join a local network group; the following information provides guidelines for networking if a group doesn't exist in your locale. If you need more help, colleges provide counseling; talk with a career advisor at your alma mater or a local college. Job-hunting manuals offer good advice.

Once you have a career objective in mind you are ready to set about reaching those who have the jobs. A network is the system through which you tell others what you have to offer as well as find out about available jobs and the going salaries in your field.

Perhaps you've planned your career with a particular corporation or profession in mind. If so you're several steps ahead. If you haven't set your sights on a specific job, or if you need to focus a broad range of job experiences, one of your first steps is to find out more about potential employers who can use your skills. If you aren't sure who they are, go to a local library and research corporations and their primary services or products. Match your skills to the company's needs. Check through the yellow pages under specific listings—marketing, for example—and match your expertise with the companies listed. Make a practice of glancing through the employment section of the daily paper to get an idea of the jobs available in your area. If you see a job listing or a company that interests you, call or write and ask for the name of the person who heads the particular job or division you're interested in. For example, if you're interested in a vacancy in the public relations division, speak to the person in charge of that area.

If you can't get through to the head person, simply ask the secretary for the name, title, and correct address. Follow up with a letter that lists your main qualifications for the job. Include a resume if doing so strengthens your case. After ten days, call the company and ask to speak directly with the person to whom you sent the letter and resume. Be persistent but not offensive. If the secretary tells you the person isn't available, leave your name and telephone number. Most executives will speak with you or will return your call. That's the appropriate time to ask for an interview.

If you're put off, ask when you can call back for an interview.

Keep a card file of names, telephone numbers, and contact dates. Eventually you'll land an interview, and a job.

When promoting a new product, market experts don't simply approach consumers at large. They target a *select public,* a public that has tested the product and now will pass its benefits on. Product promotion experts first introduce their products to those who influence others. Take their lead: focus on those who can advance and promote your career. Study your associates and determine which ones are likely to know your professional capabilities. Keep in touch with them regularly to let them know your changing career objectives.

You are at the center of numerous relationships, some business, others strictly social. Think about the people you spend time with and decide how important they are to your personal and professional growth. Ask yourself these questions: Who are the people I come in contact with on a regular basis? Where do I spend most of my time and energy? To get an idea, list your social and business acquaintances and keep a log of how much time you spend with each, what you do together, and whether you're benefiting from the relationship. Time spent with friends who offer little beyond a good time is entertaining, but a dead end for your career.

Build quality professional relationships. Set priorities among associates. It's just as easy and more worthwhile in the long run to lunch with an associate who shares your career goals than it is to eat with someone who isn't interested in advancing. A main objective is to keep in touch with influential people who can help you advance.

Establish a relationship with a mentor, someone in your business life whom you trust and look up to for guidance. Sometimes it's nice just to have someone to talk to. Select someone you respect, someone more seasoned in the business world, someone whose character and career development you can emulate. Be careful to choose someone who will feel honored when you ask advice.

There are other media than the telephone that you can use for self-promotion. The objective is recognition: get your name in the limelight. For example, contribute an article to the corporate newsletter or quarterly report. Get involved; attend departmental meetings in which decisions are made. Volunteer for committees that decide corporate policy. Sit in on corporate board meetings. Volunteer to work at a shareholders' gathering.

Self-promotion need not be limited only to the place you work. Developing yourself and your reputation outside the office shows interest in total professional growth.

Memberships in professional associations fill you in on what other professionals in your field are doing and keep you abreast of official happenings. Professional associations hold monthly luncheons or meetings which include panel discussions and speeches by experts in the field. Join a panel or volunteer to speak—you will meet other experts and increase your credentials. Run for election and serve as an officer of the association. If you join several business groups, you will meet people who can help you find a new job when you want to change.

Volunteer for political campaigns or community service projects such as fund raising for a hospital. You will gain valuable experience while meeting influential civic leaders. Volunteering is good for the career changer because it gives first-hand experience and contacts in fields other than your own.

Part-time jobs also can set a career change in motion. One client, working in newspaper advertising, wanted to switch into radio advertising. She began her career change by working part-time for a radio station. She learned the ropes and made a contact who offered her a full-time job.

Additional education and training is a life long demand in some careers. When you attend seminars and classes, you meet people with interests and backgrounds similar to yours while learning useful skills. You get a chance to meet instructors and guest lecturers who are recognized experts.

Write articles for the corporate newsletter, magazine, or annual report. Submit articles to trade and association journals. A published article garners favorable recognition of your name. If your article isn't published, be sure your superiors know that you tried; they will appreciate the fact that you made an attempt. Show your boss the article, and keep trying.

Research newspapers, magazines, and newsletters for features about prominent business leaders. Don't be afraid to send them a resume or contact their office. Many job searches come to a satisfactory conclusion because the job seeker contacted a prominent corporate executive and expressed interest in a job.

Collect business cards. On the back of the card, make notes about the person, the place you met, and your conversation.

Start a contact file, based on the cards you collect and the profiles taken from newspapers and magazines. Complete a three-by-five note card on each person, and keep it in a ready reference file. The file not only will help your job hunt, but also serves your present job as a mailing list and as a compendium of valuable business contacts.

Join a network group. They exist in most major cities. Women's career centers publish newsletters and magazines; reading them provides information on who is doing what. The newsletters welcome contributions. Don't overlook the value of socializing with the group. You make contacts and need not become a name dropper.

Self-Promotional Aids

A second means of self-promotion are materials that reflect professional style. Clients often ask my advice about correct business card or stationery format. The following guidelines will help. Print shops offer greater detail. Note that guidelines are given for setting up a portfolio, and that resumes are not included. They're omitted because individual styles and needs vary greatly. There are also numerous manuals on how to write a resume.

Business cards. Business cards create a professional image by saying that you are important enough to warrant special identification. They show that you know the value of keeping in touch. They increase visibility because contacts are more likely to recall your name and may include your card in a ready reference file or mailing list.

Follow these guidelines and refer to Figure 11-1.

1. Your name, title, corporation name, address, and telephone number should be listed. Sales and regional service reps often include their home address and telephone number if they don't mind being reached at home.

2. Include a corporate or organization logo or other identifier, preferably in color or raised letters.

3. Keep business cards small and simple to fit easily into a wallet or purse. More dramatic designs are acceptable in the creative professions. Otherwise be conservative.

4. Colored paper is acceptable.

Business or personalized stationery. Many new business or small business owners such as consultants or sales representatives need help in selecting or designing stationery. Acceptable business stationery adds to the prestige of a beginning business. Don't scrimp on your stationery. It is often one of the first important impressions you make. (See Figure 11-2.)

Figure 11-1. **The business card.**

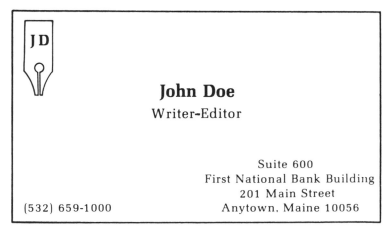

Figure 11-2. **Business or personalized stationery.**

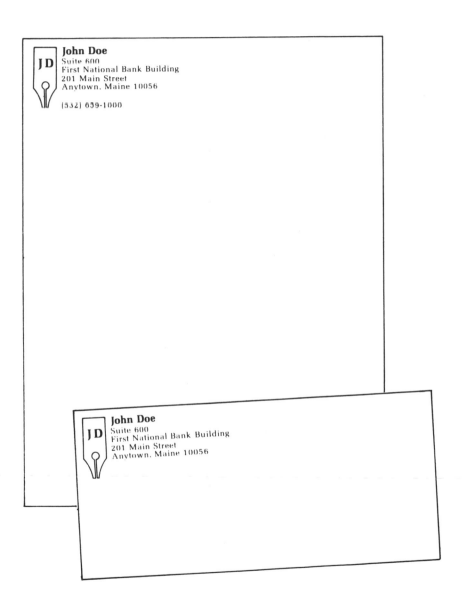

1. Choose a logo or identifier that reflects the nature of your business. For example, a free-lance writer might choose a scroll. This may call for some creativity, and you may wish to have a creative artist or design person come up with a unique and appropriate design. To cut the expense of stationery, you can make your own logo. Printers often have a catalog of ready-made designs. It's important to carry your identifier throughout your business.

2. If you select colored stationery, don't deviate too much from the standard white bond. Cream or light ivory work well. Avoid bright colors unless you're in a very creative profession. Quality and conservatism are your best bets. Choose a reasonably heavy-grade paper; a 25–50 percent cotton bond is adequate in most cases.

3. Have the name, address, and telephone number of your business printed on the stationery. Your name and title are optional as they are ordinarily typed on anyway. Placement of your address and phone number depends on the overall design. The usual location is at the top of the sheet with the logo.

4. Envelopes should match the paper grade and color. In the upper left-hand corner, place your logo and your business name and address only.

Portfolios. Artists, photographers, and other creative professionals have long used portfolios to display samples of their work. A portfolio is a portable case filled with visual materials and other documents that attest to your career achievements. (See Figure 11-3.) Professionals outside the artistic careers find they can assemble and use a portfolio to strengthen their impression. Entering a job interview or sales meeting with a portfolio in hand gives you a distinct advantage. You have something to talk about, you have a display of your worth, and you feel more credible. Portfolios are an excellent resource for organizing, displaying, and keeping track of career growth.

To assemble a portfolio:

1. Go to a business supply store and purchase a bound portfolio case, usually zippered. Prices vary; choose a durable one. Buy perhaps a rainproof case in vinyl with clear insertion sheets

Figure 11-3. **The portfolio.**

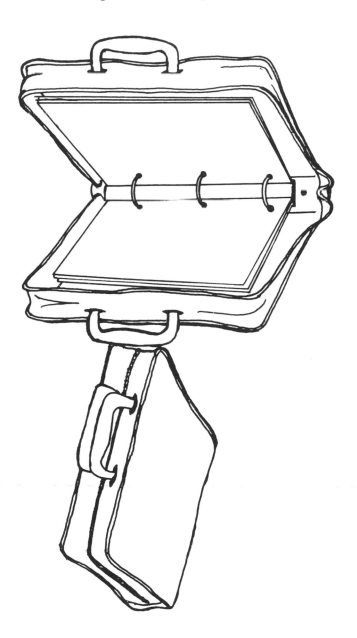

inside. Most business supply stores can recommend an appropriate one.

2. Select a size that's easy to handle and that you feel comfortable carrying around.

3. Insert light-colored construction paper inside the clear sheets to add visual interest. Display your articles, awards, resume, etc. chronologically against this background. Make sure each item you include is relevant and easily identified. For example, people in advertising would include samples of brochures, flyers, and ads they've worked on.

4. Photographs and work samples make the most interesting and relevant display.

As you advance in your career, add to your portfolio anything that shows career growth. If you're just starting, include relevant college research papers, studies, speeches you worked on, and summaries of internship projects. If you're a more established professional, include magazine or newspaper articles. The small business owner might include samples of important jobs completed for clients. Letters of recommendation are good insertions. Samples of your work are a must.

(12)

Image in the Job Interview

Most people enter a job interview feeling apprehensive, and as a result they appear nervous and lose their ability to come across as a confident, well-qualified professional. Recall that those you meet in the business and professional world form their lasting impression within the first thirty seconds after meeting you, making the need to create a confident image immediately even more important. An interview is usually an interpersonal, one-to-one exchange. As a job applicant, you are in close contact with another person who observes your every move.

An interview serves several purposes for you: to gather information, to give information, and to persuade or be persuaded. In the true sense of the word, you're selling yourself, and the prospective employer is buying your abilities and skills.

Preparation Helps Overcome the Fear

Don't walk into an interview blind. Find out as much about the company, the job, and the types of people who already work there as you can. It's too late six months down the road to decide you don't like your job or the company.

Research the company. Write or telephone for a corporate manual or annual report that describes the company's standing in the community and its potential for growth. Pay special attention to the corporate philosophy, the product or service, and the number of years in business. Go to the local library and read the Better Business Bureau rating. Research serves two purposes. First, you go into the interview prepared to ask questions that show your interest and knowledge about the company. Second, for several years or more, its future becomes your future. Research into the company helps you eliminate poor risks.

The job search, including the interview, is a time of decision; you are choosing a job that will take up several years of your life. You want to make sure to go with a company that can use your talents. The usual attitude of job seekers is that it's their duty to persuade a prospective employer that they are a good investment. There's another side. The applicant has invested time and money in acquiring skills, experience, and education. The investment is wasted by accepting a job that does not put the potential to good use. Give a lot of thought to how a job can advance your career before accepting it.

Find out who will be interviewing you, if possible. Will it be one person from the personnel department, a supervisor from the department you'll be working in, or will you talk to a vice president or manager? You can usually find out who will interview you by calling and asking the person who sets up the appointment. If not, prepare for someone from personnel or a department head.

Find out as much about the specific job as you can. If feasible, telephone someone already working in a similar slot. Ask about job duties, the boss, and any other subjects you feel are significant. You can call someone in the job you are interviewing for without being offensive; just say that you're updating your resume and want to keep them informed, or you're working on a job description manual and you need to know what the job entails. Job surveys repeatedly seek to match skills and job requirements. Some companies provide applicants with a job description. Libraries sometimes carry a directory of a company's job titles and job requirements.

Make a list of "ready identifiers" to help you get across your qualifications, overcome fear, and project a self-assured image. The objective is to compile a list of assets that are most needed in the job. When you're conversing with an interviewer who doesn't know you or your qualifications, it is your duty to build a favorable impression. With a list of a dozen ready identifiers of your strongest assets to base your discussion on, you'll feel more comfortable. Working from your list, write out an introductory statement that describes your qualifications. Keep this statement handy as your profile.

Create your list, in this format:

I. My strongest asset is: (e.g., my ability to manage)
   A. I gained it . . .
      1. As supervisor, Marcus Corporation for 4 years
      2. As manager, Stonefield Industries for 1 year
II. My second strongest asset is:
   A. I gained it . . .
      1.
      2.

And so on.

Another exercise that helps is to create a list of questions you expect to be asked. Questions usually center around how you learned about the job and why you feel you're qualified; you're usually given a typical job problem and asked how you would handle it. Role play with your spouse or a friend. Let them quiz you; knowing the topics you're likely to discuss creates a confident and knowledgeable feeling. Interviewers respect those who ask questions and those who have good answers.

Attitude. The attitude you show expresses your self-image and your self-esteem. The person interviewing you will be on the lookout for a healthy attitude. For a boost, re-read Chapter 3 on self-image. The interviewer gauges your attitude by your appearance and the way you answer questions. Your responses should be direct and sincere, not withdrawn or evasive; be assertive but not aggressive.

Express feelings openly without becoming too personal. For example, "Yes, my experience includes exposure to computers, but I've never worked directly with computer keypunch."

Be responsive. Actively participate in the interview. Establish rapport with the interviewer as soon after the interview begins as you can, preferably in an introductory statement about your interest in the company and the job. Rapport should be set by the time you shift into discussing your qualifications.

Dishonesty shows up sooner or later. Do not falsify records or make up answers. If you don't know an answer, admit it. You gain respect by admitting that you're not sure but would like to find out. Appearing to have an answer for everything weakens credibility.

Ability to listen. One of the most sought-after qualities in a manager or supervisor is the ability to listen. It shows interest and concern for others, and it may be at the top of the list of the qualities the company is looking for. Listen with both ears open; if you don't understand a question or a point, don't hesitate to ask for it to be repeated, or for clarification.

Body behavior during the interview. A slow, evenly paced entrance and exit indicate confidence. Practice a firm handshake, which indicates sincerity; no limp wrist and no bear grips. A special note to women: unless you're meeting another woman, it is usually expected that you extend your hand first.

Whether you are standing or seated, an erect, comfortable posture shows interest, sincerity and attentiveness. When asking or responding to direct questions, lean slightly toward the interviewer to indicate confidence in asking or willingness to respond.

When seated, don't squirm. Avoid scuffing the feet, which shows tension. It's acceptable for men and women to cross their legs at the knee. Practice seated posture before going to the interview by sitting in a chair and moving around until you find a comfortable position. Cross your legs at the knee and then at the ankle. Which feels natural? Place your hands in your lap, with hands extended out toward the interviewer.

Maintain eye contact for 80 to 95 percent of the time. Direct eye contact shows interest and confidence; it signals that you're listening. Extended eye contact can dominate. To avoid intimidation, break the contact by looking slightly away from the interviewer occasionally.

Don't squirm, but don't sit perfectly still either. Some animation increases interest and credibility. An occasional shift in position is also relaxing. Vary the posture, for example, by leaning forward toward the interviewer when responding, and assuming an erect, attentive posture when listening. Use some hand gestures but don't overdo them. Hands extended out to the interviewer draws attention to you.

In voice, be expressive and speak loudly and clearly enough to be heard and understood. Don't be afraid to speak up, and articulate your words. If you can't be understood, you convey an unconfident image. Speak at a rate that makes your words easy to understand. Re-read Chapter 7 for details about overcoming a specific vocal image problem.

Use of language. The way you express yourself includes your vocabulary. Avoid slang and triteness. Use good grammar and don't try to impress the interviewer with an "educated" vocabulary. The believable and sincere person speaks on the level of the interviewer. Familiarize yourself with appropriate business language and special terminology used in the particular corporation or career you are trying to enter. For example, if you're interviewing for a job in a company that sells computers, familiarize yourself with basic computer terms.

How to dress. Specific guidelines for conveying an authoritative, sincere image with wardrobe are given in Chapter 4. Reread it for details.

Bear in mind that different professions and corporations have different expectations about what is appropriate in dress. A designer label might be appropriate for a job in fashion but out of place for a job in industry, banking, or other conservative calling. Faddish clothes such as blue jeans, even when worn with a white shirt and blazer, are not acceptable job interview gear. Clothes indicate to the interviewer whether you're taking the job in order to work or to play. You don't get a second chance; you cannot undo a wrong first impression.

Interview setting. The time of day when the interview is conducted, and the office or room where it takes place are important to consider. If you're at your best in the afternoon, try to schedule an appointment then. If you walk in half asleep, you're at an immediate disadvantage. There's usually some scheduling leeway. If the time you want is not convenient for the interviewer, agree to the suggested schedule.

Be prepared for the office where you'll be interviewed. Review Chapter 8 as a guide for levels of authoritative positioning in an office. Keep in mind the arrangement of the interview room, and seating patterns in particular, can create intimidation and control of you. Try to avoid arrangements that diminish your impact. For example, don't sit on a large sofa unless the interviewer chooses a seat away from the desk. Instead, choose a single seat closer to the desk. A large, comfortable sofa swallows you up, and your authority too.

The Image of the Interviewer: Guidelines

The same general rules regarding attitude and physical appearance apply for an interviewer and a job seeker. As the leader of the interview, you're expected to make the applicant feel at ease; it's up to you to carry the ball and draw out information.

Do your homework. Find out as much about the applicant as you can prior to the first encounter by reading over the resume several times.

Since you're expected to lead the interview, be familiar with correct interview format. Like speeches, interviews should be broken into an opening, a body and a closing. Design the opening questions to put the applicant at ease. For example, start out discussing a common interest or hobby, and proceed in the main body of the

Figure 12-1. **Informal, relaxed setting for a job interview.**

interview to serious questions that uncover job qualifications. Your job also includes explaining departmental and corporate philosophy and requirements, detailing the superiors to report to, and outlining salary and promotion potential. Pause often for questions. Close by summing up the discussion and asking for further questions. Give the applicant a definite date by which to expect to hear from you about the hiring decision.

Arrange the setting in a less intimidating and less authoritative pattern than usual. For example, leave your desk and sit with the interviewee in two chairs, or in a sofa and chair arrangement. (See Figure 12-1.) Re-read Chapter 8 for guidelines about seating arrangements.

Additional Suggestions

1. Take the initiative in getting the interview underway. Don't just sit and stare at the applicant entering the room. Offer your hand first. Ask the interviewee to take a seat and establish rapport before probing about skills and qualifications.

2. Make a casual, smooth transition from the opening remarks to the first serious topic of the interview. Start off with a welcoming statement: "It's nice to meet you. How did you find out about our company?" Proceed to questions about the applicant's background. Encourage response by asking questions such as, "I notice you have an interest in writing and that you've published several articles. How do you feel your writing experience would help you in our job in public relations?"

3. Listen as much as you talk. Prompt the applicant to talk by interjecting "yes" or "go on" frequently.

4. Don't exaggerate the benefits of the company or the job. Be honest about potential for growth in the corporation and in the job.

5. Without appearing overly regimented, structure the interview so that you avoid jumping around. Don't give the impression that you're conducting an all-out investigation, but don't ramble, either.

6. Be alert to the applicant's answers and behavior. Pick up on the cues that are logical breaks for asking a question, changing the topic, or drawing out the applicant further.

7. Ask questions that uncover the applicant's attitudes and personality. Gear the questions to job or corporate demands. For example, "In your job you'd have direct public contact. If you have twenty people waiting and it's time to close the office, how would you handle the situation?"

8. Keep in mind that an open, trusting attitude is called for in an interview. If you as an interviewer project an open, sincere image, you create the proper atmosphere and set the right pace.

Index

AMACOM Paperbacks

John Fenton	The A To Z Of Sales Management	$ 7.95	07580
Hank Seiden	Advertising Pure And Simple	$ 7.95	07510
Alice G. Sargent	The Androgynous Manager	$ 8.95	07601
John D. Arnold	The Art Of Decision Making	$ 6.95	07537
Oxenfeldt & Miller & Dickinson	A Basic Approach To Executive Decision Making	$ 7.95	07551
Curtis W. Symonds	Basic Financial Management	$ 7.95	07563
William R. Osgood	Basics Of Successful Business Planning	$ 7.95	07579
Dickens & Dickens	The Black Manager	$10.95	07564
Ken Cooper	Bodybusiness	$ 5.95	07545
Richard R. Conarroe	Bravely, Bravely In Business	$ 3.95	07509
Jones & Trentin	Budgeting	$12.95	07528
Adam Starchild	Building Wealth	$ 7.95	07594
Laura Brill	Business Writing Quick And Easy	$ 5.95	07598
Rinella & Robbins	Career Power	$ 7.95	07586
Andrew H. Souerwine	Career Strategies	$ 7.95	07535
Beverly A. Potter	Changing Performance On The Job	$ 9.95	07613
Donna N. Douglass	Choice And Compromise	$ 8.95	07604
Philip R. Lund	Compelling Selling	$ 5.95	07508
Joseph M. Vles	Computer Basics	$ 6.95	07599
Hart & Schleicher	A Conference And Workshop Planner's Manual	$15.95	07003
Leon Wortman	A Deskbook Of Business Management	$14.95	07571
John D. Drake	Effective Interviewing	$ 8.95	07600
James J. Cribbin	Effective Managerial Leadership	$ 6.95	07504
Eugene J. Benge	Elements Of Modern Management	$ 5.95	07519
Edward N. Rausch	Financial Management For Small Business	$ 7.95	07585
Loren B. Belker	The First-Time Manager	$ 6.95	07588
Whitsett & Yorks	From Management Theory to Business Sense	$17.95	07610
Ronald D. Brown	From Selling To Managing	$ 5.95	07500
Murray L. Weidenbaum	The Future Of Business Regulation	$ 5.95	07533
Craig S. Rice	Getting Good People And Keeping Them	$ 8.95	07614
Charles Hughes	Goal Setting	$ 4.95	07520
Richard E. Byrd	A Guide To Personal Risk Taking	$ 7.95	07505
Charles Margerison	How To Assess Your Managerial Style	$ 6.95	07584
S.H. Simmons	How To Be The Life Of The Podium	$ 8.95	07565
D. German & J. German	How To Find A Job When Jobs Are Hard To Find	$ 7.95	07592
W.H. Krause	How To Get Started As A Manufacturer's Representative	$ 8.95	07574
Sal T. Massimino	How To Master The Art Of Closing Sales	$ 5.95	07593